SPECTACULAR KITCHENS TEXAS

INSPIRING KITCHEN AND DINING SPACES
Jolie Carpenter

Published by

www.signatureboutiquebooks.com

Publisher: Jolie M. Carpenter
Publisher: Brian G. Carabet
Graphic Designer: Laura Greenwood
Managing Editor: Rosalie Wilson
Editors: Katrina Almendarez, Amber Bell, Lori Tate,
Rachel Watkins, Megan Winkler
Associate Publishers: Courtney Williams, Hedy Vanderheyden
Art Director: Morganne Stewart

Printed in Malaysia

Distributed by Independent Publishers Group
800.888.4741

PUBLISHER'S DATA

Spectacular Kitchens of Texas

Library of Congress Control Number: 2015915185

ISBN 13: 978-0-9964240-0-4
ISBN 10: 0-9964240-0-8

First Printing 2016

10 9 8 7 6 5 4 3 2 1

Right: Overland Partners, page 131
Previous Page: Palmer Todd, page 137

Signature Publishing Group is dedicated to the restoration and conservation of
the environment. *Spectacular Kitchens of Texas* was manufactured with strict
adherence to an environmental management system in accordance with ISO
14001 standards, including the use of paper from mills certified to derive their
products from environmentally managed forests. We are committed to continued
investigation of alternative paper products and environmentally responsible
manufacturing processes to ensure the preservation of our fragile planet.

INTRODUCTION

What makes a kitchen spectacular? We combed the state and found the most talented design professionals in Texas and asked them to showcase their favorite kitchens to help us answer that question. On the following pages, you will see a variety of styles of gorgeous kitchens and the eye-catching spaces around them. You won't get to meet the homeowners, though you will get a sense of who they are simply by touring the heart of their home. A kitchen, like any space in a home, is very personal and it tells a story. I had the privilege of accompanying many of the artisans into their works of art, and it was obvious to me what kind of people lived in the spaces—the animal lovers with dog beds sprinkled around, the big family with artwork on the fridge, the entertainer with tons of seating and a huge dining table. Every home was interesting in its own unique design. The kitchen space was always determined by the needs, lifestyle, and budget of the dwellers. And the artistry is impressive. The professionals behind the designs are the dream-makers and the producers of every detail that results in the dazzling kitchen spaces you'll see in this book. A heartfelt thank you goes out to everyone whose work is displayed in this collection, not only are they uber-talented, they are a group of laidback, kind, and friendly people who I thoroughly enjoyed working with! Many of them have contributed their work in several of my previous books and become friends and trusted collaborators—for that I am eternally grateful. It's because of these industry leaders that I have a platform to continue to produce beautiful books that inspire.

One thing I learned as I produced this book is that size and scale do not equal spectacular. I found that regardless of square footage or price point, every kitchen has its unique personality and function designed for its purpose, whether it's for the avid cook, the busy family, or the bachelor in a high-rise. I am a cook and I throw a lot of dinner parties, so the kitchens with the most extravagant appliances appealed to me, particularly the ones with beautifully displayed wine storage. In fact, I was motivated to add a few design elements to my own kitchen—I had some white linen roman shades made and I added some black and white linen stools to my bar. As you can see in the picture here, my kitchen is small, so these tasteful additions made a huge impact.

Whatever your design preference, I'm certain you will find inspiration from the variety of gorgeous kitchen spaces in this curated collection of irresistible design. We couldn't possibly print all the kitchens we love, so we are taking to social media—and what could be more spectacular than that? Check us out on the Spectacular Kitchens Facebook page and on Instagram at Signature Boutique Books, where we will keep you up to date on the latest kitchen inspiration.

All the best,

Jolie Carpenter

Jolie at home in Dallas with Charlie Boy.
Photo by Danny Piassick who found Charlie Boy his happy
new home where he is the center of attention in Jolie's kitchen.

CONTENTS

Photographs feature the design of Emily Seiders of Studio Seiders Tile and Design
TOP LEFT Photograph by Ryann Ford
TOP RIGHT Photograph by Jessica Pages Photography
FACING PAGE LEFT Photograph by Carl Mayfiled
FACING PAGE RIGHT Photograph by Jessica Pages Photography

7

JEIDesign, page 35

Jon Luce Builder, page 39

Architectural
Granite & Marble

Nature is the best inspiration for timeless design.

Architectural Granite & Marble carries on a family legacy. Jack Seiders founded the stone supplier in 1992; his son Chad continues to foster the long-term relationships the company has built up with its clientele. The firm's mission is to supply homeowners with the highest quality natural stones of the world. From natural stone tile, granite, marble, soapstone, and travertine—in slabs or cut-to-size—the depth and breadth of selection is unmatched. Partners in Brazil, China, Italy, and India professionally inspect each slab before sending it to the supplier, and the fabricators' facilities receive thorough examination as well. Headquartered in Austin, AG&M has expanded to San Antonio and Oklahoma City as well as North Carolina and Tennessee over the years. Wandering the showroom, potential buyers can peruse the entire inventory and utilize cutting-edge technology to visualize selections in a virtual kitchen. An on-site design team offers convenient consulting, and on-premise slab yards allow for up-close inspection of choices. The stone experts' passion is infectious, and homeowners find it hard not to get excited.

LEFT: The exquisite marble feature wall and waterfall island demonstrate that a single material used brilliantly can create a dramatic effect.
Photograph by Robert Reck Photography

Arete European Kitchens

Attention to detail without exception is critical to design success.

Great design isn't about just one fabulous idea; it's the culmination of numerous products and philosophies that all work together to create something bigger. Design firm Arete European Kitchens shows this in every one of its luxury projects, as top-notch products come from German manufacturers like Leicht, Alno, and Miele, that take pride in the precision and modernity of their work: cabinetry, fixtures, and appliances. From inception to installation, the industry veterans of Arete European Kitchens work closely with homeowners and leave no detail untouched—innovation and individuality are the focus with each project without losing sight of functionality and everyday use. Owners Tom and Andrea Wilkinson operate the design firm in Austin and use an impressive 2,500-square-foot showroom to reveal ideas and inspirations to homeowners from all over Texas. A highly skilled team of design specialists are on-hand to introduce guests to and personally guide them in discovering the endless possibilities, whether the project calls for ground-up design or partial refurbishing.

LEFT: The renovation project took cues from the original layout and purified the visual form by integrating appliances and utilizing slab fronts and minimally profiled linear handles. The kitchen's exterior function successfully balances the active family's daily undertakings and transitions to comfortably host large gatherings. In true European style, great attention is paid to details, from internal drawer lighting to unique pantry storage. Architecture by Jay Corder.
Photograph by Brian Mihealsick

Bella Vita Custom Homes

Lifestyle-inspired homes should be beautiful inside and out.

For the team at Bella Vita, beautiful homes are not just a business, they are also a lifestyle. The luxury custom home builder focuses on its clients' passions and personalities to craft homes that are reflections of the way they live. Bringing a dream to life is no small task, yet it remains one that the professionals at Bella Vita accomplish every day. After all, the company name translates as "beautiful life." Founded by four entrepreneurial construction visionaries in 2009, Bella Vita has a uniquely client-centric creative process. The future homeowners are included in every step of planning and design. They can be as involved as they would like or choose to focus on the elements that are most important to them. Clients have access to the entire team, which is an impressive roster of knowledgeable estimators, purchasers, AIA architects, ASID interior designers, construction managers, and other specialists. It's not just one person overseeing an entire project but rather a multifaceted team who care about each aspect and how everything comes together. The results are an appealing contribution to the community and an environment that fully embraces the characteristics envisioned from the very start.

LEFT: The dramatic, masonry arch ceiling creates the perfect space for state-of-the-art conveniences that are designed to be always within reach.
Photograph courtesy of Bella Vita Custom Homes

KITCHEN INSPIRATION

MOST SURPRISING KITCHEN DESIGN?
The "white kitchen" has moved into mainstream, and design-forward clients are incorporating gray as the new standard.

MOST UNUSUAL REQUEST?
An appliance garage that was so large it extended into the actual garage.

CREATIVE WAYS TO CUSTOMIZE A KITCHEN?
Hidden outlets purposely placed, unique and creative backsplashes, and pops of color. To go a step further, use all the drawers on the lower cabinets and no doors to allow complete access to the back of every cabinet. Additionally, it is more aesthetically pleasing with the horizontal lines the drawer reveals. When your kitchen caters to you, it is done right.

TOP RIGHT: From the hand-scraped red oak wood floors to the custom-built specialty cabinets, the gourmet kitchen displays exquisite craftsmanship.

BOTTOM RIGHT: Both stylish and efficient, the kitchen features Supreme Fantasy granite countertops, custom vent hood insert over a 60-inch range top, double oven, warming drawer, and paneled Viking appliances.

FACING PAGE: The kitchen at Bella Vita's Westlake Model Home provides ample storage with open counter space to allow hosts to prepare delicious meals while simultaneously entertaining their guests.
Photographs courtesy of Bella Vita Custom Homes

Chioco Design

The more information, the better the design solution.

For Jamie Chioco, kitchens act as the heart of the home for family and friends while serving as the dependable mainstay for meals and mingling. As such, they must be carefully considered and thoughtfully designed in order to maximize both style and substance. Achieving this precise balance is what Jamie and his Austin-based firm, Chioco Design, do best, as they listen to clients' unique needs and explore every facet of how they live before creating a cohesive plan. Jamie built his firm by stressing communication and collaboration between client, designer, and builder, each of which is essential to successfully achieve a well-executed, shared vision. Functional, inviting, and honest design is at the core of every Chioco Design project—from private residences to commercial spaces including restaurants, bars, and retail. What unites them is a distinctive materials palette that artfully combines man-made and natural elements while maintaining a purposeful connection to the surrounding environment. Jamie's work is driven by the opportunity to investigate the latest technology, materials, and building techniques while creatively incorporating them into the language of each new design project.

KITCHEN INSPIRATION

MOST ECONOMICAL WAY TO MAKE THE BIGGEST IMPACT?
We like to use inexpensive materials and detail them in an interesting or unexpected way. Also, keep the materials palette to a minimum for a more cohesive look.

EVERY KITCHEN DESIGN MUST INCLUDE…
Good lighting. We begin with trying to infuse the space with a balanced level of natural light then incorporate task and accent lighting, which are essential for a kitchen to function and to highlight specific architectural elements.

CREATIVE WAYS TO CUSTOMIZE A KITCHEN?
All kitchens have some version of the standard requirements and appliances, but it's the custom details that really make a space special. In one particular kitchen, we designed the bar top out of a single slab of walnut with a live edge—its natural characteristics provide a contrast to the rest of the kitchen.

TOP RIGHT: The kitchen island holds the sink and appliances while providing an all-purpose space for casual meals, studying, and entertaining. The open floorplan helps facilitate large family gatherings.

BOTTOM RIGHT: Full-height, vertical grain white oak cabinets define the kitchen area while a simple palette of white painted cabinets, horizontally coursed marble tile, and walnut floors provide warmth and texture.

FACING PAGE: Daylight filters through the custom cabinet designed to display the client's glass collection. Dark soapstone counters contrast with the white painted cabinets and stainless steel accents.

PREVIOUS PAGES: Natural light from multiple locations helps to create an even daylighting level. Walnut cabinetry and a soapstone bar define the kitchen area.
Photographs by Casey Dunn

Dick Clark + Associates

The best design solutions are holistically developed.

A veritable think tank for creative designs, Dick Clark + Associates has been sharing its brand of holistic collaboration with Austin for the better part of four decades. The education and experience of the firm's leadership reaches from Los Angeles to Boston and as far away as Central America and Europe. The firm's equally diverse body of work is a testament to the professionals' forward-thinking mentality and dedication to developing truly site-specific designs. Whether residential or commercial, new construction or renovation, the firm's dynamic staff of architects and interior designers provide solutions that are conceived at once, yielding a wonderfully cohesive, polished look. Though DC+A has a serious portfolio, the studio's atmosphere is fun and casual, providing an environment where everyone can do his or her best work. The highly collaborative environment balances the aesthetic with the functional, while providing an exceptional level of service.

TOP LEFT: Contemporary white glass cabinets and Miele appliances highlight a modern great room.
Photographs by Alex Stross

BOTTOM LEFT: Previously a screened porch, this renovated kitchen features a classic palette of white oak and Carrera marble.
Photographs by Andrea Calo

FACING PAGE: Within an urban loft, the Valcucine kitchen and Elica Ola vent hood stand as objects of art, well-suited to the owner's contemporary collection.
Photographs by Paul Bardagjy

Don Crowell Builders

There's nothing quite like a Texan spin on design.

Meaningful design stands out from the crowd, and there's something uniquely meaningful about each of the homes with which Don Crowell Builders is involved. From renovation projects to homes built from the foundation up, the distinctly cosmopolitan style of Don Crowell and his team is a treat to the eye. As principal of Don Crowell Builders, Don is committed to the highest standards of work. His integrated team of energetic project managers, who hail from backgrounds that include everything from art history and psychology to business management and accounting, create homes with a careful attention to detail that take place, historical context, and materials into consideration. The result is a diverse portfolio that emulates the artistic adventurism of the Austin region. Even the most elegantly understated home breaks the mold—the team loves allowing a home to reveal its subtle charms through a thoughtful combination of materials and planning in unexpected ways.

TOP LEFT: Despite its rectilinear composition, the catering kitchen feels spacious thanks to tall cabinetry and a large window that visually expand the space.

BOTTOM LEFT: The outdoor dining area boasts expansive views and a covered walkway that invites exploration of the property.

FACING PAGE: The over-sized island expresses the homeowners' love of food and family. Fine craftsmanship makes itself known from ceiling to cabinets to floor. Calacatta marble is an elegant choice for the countertops.
Photographs by Allison Cartwright

KITCHEN INSPIRATION

BEST WAY TO BEGIN A REDESIGN?
Collaboration! We have to come together as a team both with each other and with the homeowner, architect, and interior designer to bring an idea to life. Getting everyone on the same page is essential.

FIRST THING YOU LOOK FOR WHEN DESIGNING A KITCHEN?
Beyond proper functional layout I always look for the little details—from how joints come together in the corner to the overall flow of the room. It's the little details that will make or break the design.

THOUGHTS ON REFINISHING VERSUS REPLACING?
If an element adds character to the space, by all means refinish it. There's a certain charm to elements from days gone by. Just remember that the kitchen is usually the hub of the house and demands utility. When possible, replace. Functional storage and proper fittings can completely alter the cook's experience.

RIGHT: The sophisticated, utilitarian kitchen featuring custom stainless cabinetry framing a generous soapstone slab used as the backsplash.
Photograph by Casey Dunn

FACING PAGE: Defined by a palette of warm wood, cool steel, and crisp white cabinetry, the contemporary farmhouse kitchen is oriented to take in the views. The custom dining table was built using a repurposed longleaf pine column supporting an elegant maple top.
Photograph by Casey Dunn

PREVIOUS PAGES LEFT: The traditional family gathering kitchen features an end-grain mesquite island and limestone countertops.
Photograph by Casey Dunn

PREVIOUS PAGES RIGHT: The casual, urbane kitchen abounds with artisanal details. The pewter island is an elegant counterpoint to the basalt countertops.
Photograph by Andrew Pogue

Element 5 Architecture
Good design is site-specific design.

Element 5 Architecture has a unique model. Four principal architects collaborate on every project, and one of them takes each project from start to finish—no junior staffers, no intermediaries, just the most experienced of professionals designing architecture and collaborating with clients. Nick Mehl, Jay Bolsega, Drew Randall, and Richard Hughes are experienced principal architects yet they also see themselves as advocates for their clients' needs and desires. Their counsel is as valuable as their drawings. On every project, the architects utilize three-dimensional renderings to ensure that the client loves the design and the builder knows exactly how to make it happen. The firm's work in commercial and residential sectors on projects varying from historical renovations to contemporary new builds gives the architects a rich perspective that informs everything they do. High-end residential work is a decided specialty as it affords the opportunity to create beautiful spaces that enhance people's daily lives. Beyond aesthetic and functionality, the architects prioritize sustainability because it is the right thing to do, for the earth and everyone on it.

LEFT: Substituting upper cabinets for counter-to-ceiling windows gives the kitchen a light and airy feel. The granite countertops resemble the bark on the oak trees outside.
Photograph by Fine Focus Photography

KITCHEN INSPIRATION

WORDS OF WISDOM?
When designing a kitchen, remember the basics of ergonomics and function. That may sound obvious, but with all the gadgets out there to choose from, it's easy to lose sight of the basic purpose of a kitchen: to efficiently enjoy cooking, serving, and cleaning up a good meal.

MOST LIBERATING DESIGN INNOVATION?
We love the trend of mixed materials and colors. A single space could have wall cabinets of one color, base cabinets of another, and different countertops for the island and other workspaces.

FAVORITE PART OF PRACTICING ARCHITECTURE?
The challenge of it. Architecture combines creativity, science, mathematics, and psychology all in one discipline. You could even throw a dash of philosophy in there, too.

SHOULD EVEN THE KITCHEN BE SITE-SPECIFIC?
When it makes sense, absolutely. For one home with broad views of the Hill Country, we dispensed with upper cabinets in favor of lots of windows.

ABOVE: Kitchen appliances, wall ovens, a wine refrigerator, and pantry are concealed along the side wall. Windows above and below give the upper cabinets a floating appearance.
Photograph by James Bruce Photography

FACING PAGE: White on white countertops and cabinetry put the focus on the owners' eclectic collection of colorful tea kettles and fresh fruit.
Photograph by Atelier Wong

JEIDesign

Design blends the art of inspiration with the science of organization.

The magic of the "before and after" is what has always captivated award-winning designer Julie Evans, Allied Member ASID and owner of JEIDesign, which she established in 1983. Her endless enthusiasm for the entire design process as well as her experience, diligence, and discerning eye have established her as one of Texas' top interior design professionals. Specializing in upscale residential design and project planning as well as remodeling and restoration, JEIDesign is known for skillfully interpreting clients' tastes and developing their ideas to surpass their wildest expectations. By combining the latest technology, innovative creativity, and in-depth industry knowledge with organizational and planning expertise, the firm executes inspired and well-edited interior design schemes that are wholly reflective of the people who inhabit them. Offering a complete range of interior design services, including resource and lifestyle research, design concept formation and CAD illustrations, project phase prioritizing, interpretations of construction, and space planning, JEIDesign fosters a seamless design process in which homeowners can be as involved or removed as they wish before the big "after" is revealed.

LEFT: The kitchen emanates a wonderful sense of warmth, with the beautiful wood grain on full display in the cabinetry, flooring, and trimwork. Cool-toned wall and counter surfaces amplify the effect.
Photograph by Casey Dunn

KITCHEN INSPIRATION

MOST ECONOMICAL WAYS TO MAKE THE BIGGEST IMPACT?
Make the cabinets taller, remember that a little paint goes a long way, and upgrade your appliances!

EVERY KITCHEN DESIGN MUST INCLUDE?
A well-developed plan of how the space should function.

DIFFERENT WAYS KITCHENS NEED TO FUNCTION?
Every kitchen should be designed in light of how frequently the homeowner entertains and also should take into account how many cooks are in the kitchen—literally!

BEST PLACES TO SOURCE UNIQUE ITEMS?
There are several architectural antique websites that I often visit. And 1stDibs.com can be great, too.

TOP RIGHT: The variation in wood tone from trusses and cabinetry to island and floor creates a casual vibe while preserving the look of refined elegance.

BOTTOM RIGHT: Designed for a family that loves to cook and entertain, the kitchen is central to the main living area.

FACING PAGE: Clean lines and a crisp palette establish a contemporary look. The space is organized to take advantage of the breathtaking views.
Photographs by Casey Dunn

Jon Luce Builder

The beauty of architecture is in the details.

"It's all about constructing really cool houses—some really big and some really small—but always really good and always really fun." It's as simple as that, according to Jon Luce of Jon Luce Builder who has amassed an impressive portfolio of properties over the past three decades while simultaneously cultivating a reputation as one of the premier luxury homebuilders in the Austin area. A family business, the firm boasts an established team of artisans and craftsmen who are dedicated to creating extraordinary properties in collaboration with some of the most talented residential architects. Although Jon Luce Builder homes cross the spectrum from modern contemporary designs to present-day interpretations of classical styles, they are all unified by statement-making quality that is both unique and rare for the discerning homeowner. The exclusivity of the builder's homes is maintained by the fact that only two to three properties are constructed per year.

LEFT: Clean lines, sumptuous materials, and exquisite craftsmanship combine for the ultimate in high-end contemporary design.
Photograph by Brian Mihealsick

Latigo Building and Restoration

Do it right the first time.

With an eye for detail, David Sawtelle is a builder passionate about rural Texas architecture. Whether renovating a classic structure or building from the ground up, David is mindful to reflect the local architectural flavor of the area to ensure character and authenticity in each home. He is partial to timeless designs that reflect his team's time-honored building principles. With more than two decades of building experience—both commercial and residential—David ardently guides the entire building process. This begins at the earliest phases of parcel selection and site preparation, and it extends to landscape design and installation services. He encourages native plant life, often complemented with locally quarried hardscape, and he even installs rainwater collection systems for likeminded, eco-conscious homeowners. David's holistic approach to place-making translates to his involvement in every step. Every detail receives careful consideration and meticulous execution.

LEFT: The cabinetry design offers wonderful storage capacity while visually expanding the space.
Photograph courtesy of Latigo Building and Restoration

KITCHEN INSPIRATION

MOST SURPRISING KITCHEN PROJECT?

There was an old barn sitting right where the owners wanted to build their new home. They wanted to tear it down and get rid of everything, but I couldn't very well let that happen with all the great materials just waiting to be repurposed. We used the siding for part of the kitchen interior and in other living areas. And we rewired and refinished some great 1930s tin lights—six feet in diameter, originally used to keep baby chicks warm—into really statement-making fixtures.

WHAT DO YOU LOVE ABOUT VINTAGE PIECES?

They have a history—of another time, another place, another way of life. They bring back memories and remind you of the can-do mentality that our country was founded on, when people eagerly worked with their hands to turn something old into something new and beautiful.

CREATIVE WAYS TO CUSTOMIZE A KITCHEN?

Giving a kitchen unique rooflines, interesting cabinet arrangements, or even a screened porch makes it into a place where everyone wants to gather.

TOP RIGHT: The modern treatment of the flooring creates a sense of drama within the timeless room.

BOTTOM RIGHT & FACING PAGE: The rich hues of the floor and ceiling draw attention to the kitchen's fine millwork.
Photographs courtesy of Latigo Building and Restoration

Laughlin Homes and Restoration

The Mona Lisa didn't have a blueprint.

Relationships are important to Richard Laughlin. He treats his staff and trade partners with respect and has retained the region's top talent. A third-generation and locally grown builder, Richard was voted "Man of the Year" by his hometown chamber of commerce. The team is involved with a number of charitable organizations, emphasizing a spirit of community pride. Everyone who works with Laughlin Homes appreciates the work ethic, perfectionist nature, and policy of open communication. They let homeowners know that there will be "opportunities" along the way—it's all part of the creative process—and that they love nothing more than coming up with creative solutions that push the project to the next level. Since 1984, the design-build team at Laughlin Homes and Restoration has been enhancing the beauty of the Texas Hill Country with handcrafted custom homes and historically detailed restoration projects.

LEFT: Reclaimed materials—brick, iron, and lumber—were selected for their character and to conserve natural resources. Furniture-grade cabinetry was styled around locally reclaimed apothecary casework to be functional and efficient while maintaining a simplistic historic look. The custom retro-style vent-a hood design was handcrafted by a local tinsmith. *Photograph by Blake Mistich*

LEFT: The open shelving of the butler's pantry gives the space a welcoming aesthetic and also proves to be a functional solution for having a variety of references and ingredients at the chefs' fingertips.

ABOVE: Furniture grade custom millwork, honed granite, a handcrafted stainless hood surround, and Saltillo tile floors combine for a beautiful tailored look.

FACING PAGE: In the tranquil country kitchen, upper cabinets were used sparingly on exterior walls, allowing for oversized windows that maximize views. Fine millwork, handmade tile, and salvaged timbers reflect the attention to detail found throughout the home.
Photographs by Blake Mistich

KITCHEN INSPIRATION

MAIN SOURCES OF CREATIVE INSPIRATION?
My clients are my main source of inspiration followed by the architecture and materials of the surrounding space.

EXTRAVAGANT DESIGN FEATURES TO ADD?
Natural northern light, expansive windows, clerestories or skylights that bring the outside in. I try to avoid western exposures unless protected by porches.

MOST UNIQUE WAYS YOU'VE PERSONALIZED A KITCHEN?
We've incorporated numerous salvaged items including antique apothecary cabinetry in a pharmacist's home.

TOP RIGHT: The outdoor kitchen extends the home's entertainment area out onto the covered deck. The open frame construction of the porch and use of barn wood on the outdoor kitchen complement the rugged setting and panoramic view of the river below.
Photograph by Reflections Photography

BOTTOM RIGHT: The sophisticated wine vault showcases the unique and expansive wine collection in a temperature and humidity controlled environment. The vault is a beautiful environment for entertaining.
Photograph by Reflections Photography

FACING PAGE: The expansive island anchors the understated kitchen. Antique barn siding adds warmth and texture to the space. Hand-hewn beams accent the oversized windows and doors that open onto the covered patio.
Photograph by Blake Mistich

Laura Burton Interiors

Every space should be timeless and one-of-a-kind.

The transformative power of good design is ultimately what drives Laura Burton of Laura Burton Interiors. The award-winning designer is known for her compelling use of space, where she puts her architectural background to work in stripping away the old and conceptualizing the new. Treating rooms as works of art, she reconfigures structural elements while accounting for the subtlest of details, such as the interplay of color and materials and the way in which natural light dances across a space. What most interests her is creating the opportunity for her clients to experience their vision transformed into reality. Collaborating closely on every project, she identifies the right inspiration and sensation for a space with an eye towards that which is timeless rather than trendy. For Laura, the goal is to ultimately balance optimal function with striking design form, achieving creative and unexpected solutions that truly represent her clients and their lifestyles.

LEFT: Creamy recycled-glass counters and light wood tones pair with shaker style doors and exposed beams to create an airy craftsman look. The pale blue island, light green walls, and whimsical penny tile backsplash infuse the space with color.
Photograph by Whit Preston

KITCHEN INSPIRATION

EVERY KITCHEN DESIGN MUST INCLUDE?
A perch for a friend! Whether it's an island with barstools, a small table with a chair, or even a stool tucked away in a corner, provide a chance for togetherness. After all, cooking is a social experience.

THOUGHTS ON REFINISHING VERSUS REPLACING?
Identify and prioritize functionality and quality, and don't spend money on Band-Aid solutions. Wait until a time when you can do it right and achieve optimal results.

MOST SURPRISING DESIGN?
An unexpected bar countertop. A client had ordered a glass bar top and it was mounted incorrectly, leaving her stuck with a giant piece of broken glass and no budget left for a replacement. She and her family are fun, artistic, and whimsical, so we commissioned an artist friend to create a piece of art for the bar top out of durable material cut to size. Now they have a conversation piece in the kitchen—and a wacky story about its origins.

LEFT: Once dark and dated, the home's new kitchen is full of life. The butterfly roof allows clerestory windows to flood the space with daylight. Vibrant accents, such as the fun orange barstools, pop against a canvas of white walls and light wood tones.
Photograph by Fine Focus Photography

BOTTOM LEFT: Texture adds visual interest to the dramatic range-top backsplash while still keeping a neutral white palette.
Photograph by Fine Focus Photography

FACING PAGE: This remodel incorporates contemporary style into traditional architecture. Featuring two islands—one for cooking and the other for gathering and conversation—the kitchen is great for entertaining large groups. The unique lighting, waterfall countertop, and textural stone backsplash steal the show in the fundamentally neutral palette.
Photograph by Casey Dunn

Lawrence Construction

Confidence and trust are the cornerstones of a great relationship.

Few professions yield the satisfaction of physically creating something. This is what first drew Roger Lawrence to the construction industry and, more than three decades later, he still feels that genuine enthusiasm for his craft. Drawing on his experience while staying abreast of the latest building materials and methodologies, Roger and his team can always come up with creative options to solve unique challenges. And prospective clients of Lawrence Construction feel confident that they can trust in Roger's experience. His ability to help clients think three-dimensionally and envision the completed project, whether it's ground-up construction or a more straight forward remodel, instills that confidence and allows the client to share in the excitement. Among his more rewarding rooms are the kitchens he creates, since so much special family time is shared there. Roger's integrity, easy way of interacting with his clients, and attention to detail are exemplified in the completed project, and homeowners trust that the end result will be a space that their family will love to share.

LEFT: The working kitchen expansion and remodel was designed for a professional dessert chef. One of her favorite features is the Carrara marble slab embedded in the concrete counter.
Photograph by Coles Hairston

KITCHEN INSPIRATION

TOP CONSTRUCTION CONSIDERATION?
The most important thing for homeowners to keep in mind is the timeline. Everybody needs to be on the same page about how long the project will take.

COMMON CONVERSATIONS?
People often have preconceived notions about the cost of the project. Our job is to ask the right questions and educate clients about cost, quality, and how to get the desired results.

MOST UNUSUAL REQUESTS?
I was once asked to build a full-sized scale model of a kitchen out of cardboard so the clients could see how it would look and feel.

TOP & FACING PAGE: The modern kitchen, designed by Vicki Mayabb Interiors, features vertical grain fir cabinets with absolute black granite countertops. The spacious elevated patio and outside eating areas overlook a stunning waterfront view of Lake Travis.
Photograph by Daniel Driensky

RIGHT: The open concept in the professional kitchen, designed by Paula Ables Interiors, creates a perfect setting for both entertaining and cooking demonstrations.
Photograph by Coles Hairston

Miró Rivera Architects

Sustainability is always in style.

Artists rarely appreciate being defined by a particular look or style, but the creative minds at Miró Rivera Architects agree that their body of work is greatly informed by a sculptural approach to developing architectural forms, a sense of stewardship for the environment, and a deep connection between the natural and built worlds. These subtle signatures are what draw patrons with very unique sites and complex design requirements to the Austin-based firm. Since partnering in the late 1990s, principals Juan Miró, FAIA, and Miguel Rivera, FAIA, have collaborated on an impressive array of projects. Both give back to the architectural community by sharing their creative and technical savvy through lectures around the world. Whether designing something as high-profile as the main buildings at Circuit of The Americas, as complex as a bridge, as intimate as a private residence, or as comparatively small-scale as a new kitchen, they are thrilled at the possibilities for creative expression.

TOP LEFT: Stainless steel and subway tile maintain a balance between modern and traditional.

BOTTOM LEFT: Ipe barstools were custom designed by the architect.

FACING PAGE: The white painted walls and ceiling contrast with the dark ipe and soapstone countertops.
Photographs by Paul Finkel | Piston Design

New Life Hardwoods

Good materials get even better over time.

Centuries ago, North America was a dense primeval forest filled with giant trees that grew slowly and steadily to a majestic stature. As the land was settled and developed, thousands of forested arces were clear cut to serve unceremoniously as houses, barns, factories, and most every structure in America. While the tale of the North American forest did not have a happy conclusion, there is a modern-day company set on preserving the best of the past. The first time you hold a sample of New Life Hardwoods' reclaimed wood in your hands, you get it. There is a profound difference between new wood and reclaimed wood, and you just have to experience it for yourself to fully appreciate the inimitable quality. New Life Hardwoods' mission is to preserve history, conserve resources, and share reclaimed hardwoods as an integral part of fine design. The company has developed an impressive system for saving high-quality wood materials and breathing new life into them. Beyond merely offering fine hardwood, it aims to educate consumers on the best types of wood, characteristics of different species, selecting lifestyle-appropriate flooring, best practices for installation, and caring for hardwood so that it can be enjoyed for centuries to come.

TOP LEFT, BOTTOM LEFT, & FACING PAGE: Nothing can compare to the look and feel of wood from a tree that was a mere sapling when Columbus sailed on his voyages of discovery.
Photograph by Nick Johnson

Webber + Studio, Architects

Function, site, and structure are paramount.

Design and style are priorities when building homes, but as David Webber, AIA, principal of Webber + Studio, has found, addressing direct architectural needs with direct solutions allows functional design to emerge organically. Since 1997, Webber + Studio has designed numerous structures of varied type and scale. David and his diverse team are intrigued by all that North American architecture has to offer—from unglamorous commercial structures to folk traditions to chic modern abodes. But, function and context—where the home is located, the geography, and the history and culture of the site—play larger roles in David's timeless work, which has earned him global acclaim. The firm's expert approach can be seen as far away as Dubai, where the team designed breathtaking villas for some of the world's most discerning homeowners. David's clientele appreciates his firm's four core values of functionalism, expressionism, regionalism, and minimalism; they are the hallmarks that make Webber + Studio a coveted partner for distinctive design.

LEFT: Located on a bluff overlooking Lake Travis, the home is organized around the breathtakingly contemporary kitchen. The walnut island is a beautiful counterpoint to the stainless work surfaces and cool-toned cabinetry.
Photograph by Jacob Termansen

KITCHEN INSPIRATION

DIFFERENT WAYS KITCHENS NEED TO FUNCTION?
We're very focused on minimalism and functionality. A kitchen should be uncluttered, well-organized, and functional. One of the best ways to achieve that goal is to provide plenty of built-in storage and offer ample work surfaces. The design should work efficiently and be enjoyable to use.

FIRST THING YOU SEE WHEN STARTING A REMODELING PROJECT?
First and foremost, I look at its bones. Are there internal spaces we can create from the existing structure? Are there exterior spaces just waiting to be claimed? There's more potential waiting in some homes than one may think. Our design interventions result in warm, well designed, day-lit spaces that our clients love to inhabit.

TOP RIGHT: The floating kitchen island offers food preparation space in addition to seating for casual meals. The bookmatched marble wall functions as a backdrop, backsplash, and display shelf.
Photograph by Paul Bardagjy

BOTTOM RIGHT: From the Carrara countertops up to the ceiling, windows flood the space with natural light. The kitchen features cantilevered storage drawers and open shelving. The floors, paneling, and drawer fronts are local pecan with characteristically wild grain variation.
Photograph by Casey Dunn

FACING PAGE: With a few simple moves, an elegant and functional space emerged. Regionally prevalent solid pecan floors add warmth and connect the home with Austin. A frameless glass panel welcomes in gentle eastern light, giving a visual connection to the outdoors.
Photograph by Paul Bardagjy

Ginger Barber Interior Design, page 73

Talbot Cooley Interiors, page 87

Jane Page Design Group, page 75

Brandon Breaux Design

Good design functions well; great design has character.

For over 15 years, Brandon Breaux, principal of Brandon Breaux Design, has been an integral part of various projects throughout Southeast Texas, applying both practical experience and theoretical knowledge to high-end residential homes. From homeowners' imaginations to groundbreaking reality, Brandon offers a full range of design and construction administration services to his clientele. He never backs down from a challenge: If homeowners can dream up a concept, Brandon wants to bring it to reality. His approach is holistic, often requiring him to wear multiple hats from designer and artist to organizer, inventor, and troubleshooter. The result is a home layered with details such as coffered ceilings, custom millwork, and expansive windows that bring the outdoors in. His designs are not only beautiful, but they're also functional and reflect the historical or regional context of the home. Whether building a house from the ground up or renovating an existing residence, Brandon creates spaces that immediately evoke feelings of home.

LEFT: The classic look was achieved with a coffered ceiling, shiplap walls, and a custom hood over the range. Cabinetry that is built-in to look like furniture give the home an elegance that will be appreciated for years to come.
Photograph by Studio Laurge LLC

KITCHEN INSPIRATION

BEST WAY TO BEGIN A REDESIGN?
It's always important to walk the space with the client to review their wants and needs for the space. You really have to understand their lifestyle in context of the design.

MOST ECONOMICAL WAY TO MAKE THE BIGGEST IMPACT?
It's always best to use timeless materials. Try to avoid trends and you'll have a space that remains relevant and current for much longer.

MOST UNUSUAL REQUEST?
The most unusual request I've received would have to be raised countertop heights at 42 inches for taller homeowners. It creates odd conditions, especially where the countertops meet the appliances.

ABOVE: Natural light and efficient circulation through the downstairs were important aspects of the previously dark and dated home. The client's taste in finishes and furnishings complemented the design of the project.

RIGHT: The level of detail gives every project a custom look that exceeds expectations.

FACING PAGE: Light cabinets and countertops give an airy feel in an otherwise small work space. Natural light borrowed from adjacent rooms adds to the openness of the bar.
Photographs by Studio Laurge LLC

Ginger Barber Interior Design

Classic or modern, just keep it simple.

Ginger Barber's professional reputation is all about her natural sense of good design, her ability to pull together surprising combinations of furnishings, fabrics, and accents into a delightfully cohesive aesthetic. Ginger's talent is clear from her design portfolio as well as her beautiful boutique-showroom, The Sitting Room, located in the upscale Houston neighborhood of River Oaks. It features an ever-changing array of treasures acquired through travels across the country. Ginger's reputation is also defined by her generosity and sincere desire to help others. Her passion for interior design allows her to create beautiful environments that enhance the lives of her clients. Her other passion is working with Habitat for Horses, an equine rescue and rehabilitation non-profit organization, where she spends most weekends. With more than three decades of design experience, she has mastered the art of distilling the essence of any style to its purest form, creating interiors that are equal parts beautiful, functional, and timeless.

TOP: The look is warm yet clean with stainless steel, contemporary cabinets, and rustic elements. *Photograph by Nick Johnson*

BOTTOM: The gracious size of the islands and two peninsulas make the kitchen an easy spot to congregate during large family gatherings. *Photograph by Nick Johnson*

FACING PAGE: All the uppers were removed in favor of a soft, country feel with counters and open shelving. *Photograph by Fran Brennan*

Jane Page Design Group

Design is an artful balance, uniting technology with timeless elegance.

For Jane Page Design Group, every interior is an adventure and possesses a "life-affirming spirit of possibility." It's this vibrant sentiment that beautifully pervades every project. Founded by Jane-Page Crump in 1980, the award-winning interior design firm works throughout Houston, Austin, The Woodlands, and surrounding areas, as well as from Colorado to Maryland, bringing uncompromisingly distinctive design and unparalleled attention to detail to every property—from new construction and residential remodels to large-scale commercial projects. Jane Page Design Group nimbly navigates a range of different styles for its diverse collection of clients, yet the common denominator is the dynamic level of quality and efficiency along with a sense of enduring sophistication. Keenly in tune with every step of the design process, the group collaborates closely with the finest contractors and architects to ensure that custom work is on point and budget requirements are met. "As a designer, one of my primary goals is to exceed the expectations of clients, guiding them through the design adventure while providing the latest information needed to complete the home's interior," says Jane-Page. This attitude of excellence has led the company to become one of the most respected in the area, as Jane-Page and her team build lasting relationships on the pillars of mutual trust and respect.

ABOVE: The bar and wine room are designed to complement the adjacent formal living room. Reclaimed French oak floors ground the walnut paneling and custom cabinetry.

RIGHT: To the far left of the formal bar's display wall, an unexpected, recessed niche houses the homeowner's specialty collection of Wild Turkey decanters. It was paneled to match the other three cabinet openings, which showcase a crystal collection. The polished nickel hammered sink sparkles against the polished black countertop.

FACING PAGE: The pendant is an antique fixture perfectly selected for the space. LED strip lights highlight the wine collection, inviting guests to peer past the iron gates.

PREVIOUS PAGES: Crisp whites and creams are punctuated by the dramatic granite countertops. The beautiful backsplash and range hood create a sense of movement throughout the space.
Photographs by Julie Soefer

ABOVE, RIGHT, & FACING PAGE: Originally a Tuscan-style space, the kitchen underwent a dramatic transformation while keeping the same flooring, ceiling beams, windows, columns, sink, and kitchen cabinet frames. Through the new space plan, more modern island design, citron glass tiles, and aluminum and glass cabinet beams, a modern design emerges. The combination of Caesarstone and reclaimed butcher block countertops creates a gorgeous aesthetic that is exceptionally sustainable.
Photographs by Julie Soefer

TOP LEFT & BOTTOM LEFT: Reclaimed European white oak floors with a medium stain of blondish gray softly contrasts with the white painted cabinets. The large fixtures were appropriately selected to complement the open space and table size. A recessed block panel pedestal was designed for the breakfast table, which seats six and has a solid cast pewter top with an ornate edge. The custom chairs have a bleached gray finish, silver nail heads, and tone-on-tone fabric. Painted beams add interest to the already gracious space and continue the peaceful rhythm of the living areas.
Photographs by Mark Scheyer

TOP RIGHT: The formal dining area matches the level of elegance found throughout the home. Lighting from a variety of sources establishes an ambience of warmth.
Photograph by Mark Scheyer

FACING PAGE: Bright, warm, and inviting, the kitchen generates the heartbeat of the modern Mediterranean home. Highly functional workspace combined with custom, coastal Italian-style cabinetry brought the client's dreams to life. Reproduction blue and white tiles—a reflection of the owner's pottery collection—finish the range backsplash. An oversized window satisfies the request for an abundance of daylight. The large island with a steamer, second sink, and lots of storage was a must for the large extended family.
Photograph by Steve Chenn

KITCHEN INSPIRATION

BEST WAY TO BEGIN A REDESIGN?
The kitchen is one of my favorite rooms to design and is where memories are made. Because of the importance of the kitchen in the lives of the family members, I first discuss with the client their dreams and needs regarding the kitchen's space.

MOST SURPRISING DESIGN?
Sometimes the most surprising designs incorporate opposing elements. For a modern classic remodel, we transformed a sun-drenched kitchen by simply creating a thoughtful balance of opposites: light and dark, cool and warm, contemporary and comfortable.

CREATIVE WAYS TO CUSTOMIZE A KITCHEN?
Using interesting finish materials such as Think Glass, stainless, tambour, translucent Quartzite and onyx and incorporating a sculptural design when possible, allows us to introduce a fabulous custom element to a kitchen. Whether applied to the wall, ceiling, cabinets (or even the floor!), unique finish materials add an element of texture and richness that enhances the space.

RIGHT & FACING PAGE: The kitchen strikes a balance between elegant and dramatic with the impressive display of cabinets. The bright white finish makes the kitchen look very spacious, and the over-the-top hood, which was hand-carved from limestone, creates a refined statement. The polished marble mosaic inset over the range is exquisitely paired with quartzite countertops.
Photographs by Julie Soefer

L. Barry Davidson Architects

Details must reflect the home's concept.

Home building is a holistic process, and few people truly understand how impactful little details like windows or roof material can be to an overall design like Leslie Barry Davidson, AIA. As principal of Houston-based L. Barry Davidson Architects AIA Incorporated, Leslie delights in building and renovating homes that respond to her clients' individual personalities and lifestyles. Passionate about historical architecture since she was very young, Leslie holds a bachelor's degree in art and architectural history from Mt. Holyoke College, a bachelor's degree in architecture and a masters of architectural design and historic preservation from the University of Illinois. For more than 30 years, Leslie has been applying this passion and extensive education and experience to commercial and residential architecture. Today her focus is on residential work, and she designs all of her projects with an eye towards green architecture, working on any project for homeowners who wish to reduce environmental impact. From residences that evoke the English countryside to rustic log cabins, traditional Hill Country homes, and mid-century modern abodes, no project is too large or too small for L. Barry Davidson Architects.

TOP LEFT, BOTTOM LEFT, & FACING PAGE: Good design is about proper space planning and the specification of wonderfully textural materials.
Photographs by Miro Dvorscak MD Photography

Talbot Cooley Interiors

Innovative perfection is always the goal.

Talbot Cooley Interiors focuses on creating unique, innovative designs, where comfort and practicality parallel their beauty. Formalizing her firm in 2001, Talbot continues to explore her creativity through her work, by incorporating her custom designs into timeless settings. Talbot's portfolio ranges from contemporary to French casual to modish traditional, allowing her to satisfy each client's individual style. Her creativity is matched only by her strong work ethic and efficiency, as Talbot believes in delivering excellent service in a timely manner with every project. Focusing on quality design, her passion and joy for her work is contagious, inspiring excitement in every home. As visions are transformed into realties, and each project comes to an end, friendships are formed, and relationships continue on.

LEFT: On the island, the white calacatta marble and the weight of the rich charcoal gray create a great balance while introducing a contemporary element.
Photograph by Blake Mistich

KITCHEN INSPIRATION

EVERY KITCHEN DESIGN MUST INCLUDE?
Personal touches. Don't put things in your kitchen just because you saw it in a magazine. Think about the items that you love and that mean something to you. Incorporating those elements into a design will make you love the space even more, and as we all know, the kitchen is where families spend the most time.

CREATIVE WAYS TO CUSTOMIZE A KITCHEN?
Pare down the accessories in the space for a clean look. Plan for more than ample storage so you can put unsightly items away until you need them. Use good materials and let those materials take centerstage. That will set your kitchen apart.

BEST WAY TO BEGIN A REDESIGN?
Ask yourself how you want to use the space. Think about what you do on a daily basis. Think all the way down to where you place your keys when you walk in the door. All of those aspects contribute to good design.

TOP RIGHT & BOTTOM RIGHT: Comfortable living areas continue the refined aesthetic found throughout the home.

FACING PAGE: Open shelving, paired with the oversized steel window, provides an abundance of natural light, creating a sleek industrial element, while bringing the outside in.
Photographs by Blake Mistich

Texas Fine Home Builders

A builder's work is someone else's home.

Perhaps the strongest testament to a company's skill is the amount of advertising, or lack thereof, it requires to recruit new business. If a company doesn't resort to traditional means of advertisement then it's obviously built a strong foundation based completely on prior work and word of mouth—a powerful tool in any industry. But good reputations aren't easily earned; Texas Fine Home Builders has done so for more than a decade, building dreams one house at a time. Its trusted name has reached as far as the ears of Texas' most distinguished homeowners, including former United States Presidents. Founded in 2004 by David Stone, Texas Fine Home Builders is a recent member of the Institute of Classical Architecture & Art and serves the Houston community with top-notch contracting services. Homeowners work with the Texas Fine Home team, along with architects and designers, to drive the homebuilding process and preserve historical homes of Texas. The firm also works closely with its sister company, Texas Fine Home Services, to give homeowners a convenient option for maintenance needs. When well-executed, routine services like painting, sealing, window washing, and roof repair ensure the home remains in as good of condition as when it was originally built.

LEFT: The classically styled kitchen features a wealth of exquisitely crafted cabinetry, which serves as a backdrop for the custom range hood and island composition.
Photograph courtesy of Texas Fine Home Builders

Triangle Interiors

Life is short, so make it beautiful.

Grand estates in the countryside, chic downtown pied-à-terres, weekend retreats by the beach, floating homes—Nicole Domercq Zarr has designed them all. Whatever the locale or canvas, she delights in the opportunity to dream up timeless designs in which every detail is carefully considered. She is perhaps best known for her classical French and English interiors that possess a twist of the contemporary. That twist could come in the form of an unexpected color palette, a well-placed modern furnishing, or interesting accent pieces from another time and place. While she believes that a home's design should be restful and pleasing to the eye, she likes to keep audiences engaged, enjoying all of the stylistic elements that make a home special. Nicole's sense of style and expertise in classical design vernaculars are a tribute to the legacy of her talented mother, Paulette, who established Triangle Interiors in 1981. Then, as now, the firm creates tastefully appointed interiors that match their residents' level of taste.

LEFT: This home was a complete remodel and a true transformation. A young family of six wanted a wide open kitchen in a fresh but classic color palette. The lanterns are from Circa Lighting, the custom paint and plaster finishes were done by Segreto, and the custom concrete tiles are from Architectural Design Resource.
Photograph by Ray Perez

KITCHEN INSPIRATION

WHERE DO YOU SOURCE UNIQUE PIECES?
I love searching, so I shop all over the country. I find many things at the Round Top Antique Festival, on trips to unexpected locations, and in some of my modern sources catalogs. I'm constantly buying pieces that catch my eye or have a story, and I hold on to them for future use.

CREATIVE WAYS TO CUSTOMIZE A KITCHEN?
I've done everything from inserting an antique, monogrammed French fireback into a range hood to retrofitting all of a homeowner's sterling pieces into their own Pacific Silvercloth drawers. I love dowels behind cabinets to hang dish towels or paper towels; spice drawers; built-in espresso machines; and pop-up shelves for large mixers. The sky is the limit on what a good designer and trim carpenter can come up with.

BEST WAY TO GET THE BIGGEST IMPACT?
New countertops and splash or new cabinet doors can quickly update a tired kitchen. Soft-palette marbles, simple backsplashes, and clean-lined cabinets are fashionable and tend to make a powerful statement.

TOP RIGHT: The custom zinc range hood from Lonestar Rangehood Co. was the inspiration for the traditional 1980s kitchen remodel. To create a cheerful yet classic feel, bright fabrics from Thibaut pop against the soft calacatta marble. Pewter sconces and lanterns from Circa Lighting.
Photograph by Dan Piassick

BOTTOM RIGHT: The new construction home is anything but ordinary with pink barstools mixed with an antique table and an antique French lighting fixture. The gray sea grass rug by Stark plays off the gray veins of the Carrera countertops.
Photograph by Ray Perez

FACING PAGE: The design work began the day the homeowners purchased the lot, and every detail received careful consideration. The homeowners spend a great deal of time in the French-inspired outdoor kitchen area. Stools and antique French clock from 2 Lucy's.
Photograph by Jill Hunter, The Scout Guide Houston

Lori Caldwell Designs, page 125

Casey Roy Design, page 109

Palmer Todd, page 137

SAN ANTONIO

A-Design by Gustavo Arredondo

Lifestyles are perfected by creatively crafted design.

Rays from the Eastern rising sun. The perfect stucco finish. A butler's pantry with refrigerator drawers. All these things are of equal importance when Gustavo Arredondo begins a new project. His life's work—and passion—is designing dream homes that embody every part of a homeowner's lifestyle, from a customized bedroom layout to a farmhouse sink purposely situated beneath a window with a view. Gustavo's firm, A-Design by Gustavo Arredondo, which he established in 1997, is known for savvy design in a variety of styles, from classic Italian to elegant Tuscan, traditional French Country to rustic Texan, transitional to contemporary. Of course, there are always those custom styles for clients looking to create something distinct and out-of-the-ordinary—a challenge that Gustavo handles with enthusiasm. And technology comes into play as well, since clients are able to see their vision come to life on a screen, right down to the landscaping. Gustavo holds a bachelor's degree in architecture from Instituto Tecnológico de Estudios Superiores de Monterrey. His world travels and multi-cultural clients, who are highly concentrated in Mexico, inspire him to think creatively and bring a fresh take to the table for every home design he tackles.

LEFT: The strong masonry materials reference traditional wine cave design, inviting wine enthusiasts to linger.
Photograph by A-Design by Gustavo Arredondo

ABOVE: A soothing rhythm is established with the variety of horizontal design elements, from the lower cabinetry to the backsplash, island top, and floor.

LEFT: The custom hood treatment serves as the centerpiece in the timeless space.

FACING PAGE: Sleek cabinetry is paired elegantly with reflective flooring, counter, and backsplash surfaces. The beamed ceiling creates a sense of warmth while celebrating the gracious ceiling volume.
Photographs by A-Design by Gustavo Arredondo

KITCHEN INSPIRATION

WHAT IS KITCHEN ARCHITECTURE ALL ABOUT?
Architecture is about more than looks. Concerning individual rooms like the kitchen and the home as a whole, architecture is about cohesiveness between the exterior and interior. All design elements need to work together so the home makes sense functionally and aesthetically.

MOST IMPORTANT THING TO CONSIDER?
The homeowners' lifestyle.

WHERE TO BEGIN?
Talk to a design professional about your needs, wishes, and goals. Those elements are the foundation of the design process, which will be most successful if you're involved the whole way through.

TOP RIGHT: Carefully placed neutral tones foster a relaxed ambience with a touch of drama.

BOTTOM RIGHT & FACING PAGE: Rich in texture and detail, the open-concept space easily accommodates large groups yet is equally comfortable for the family's daily enjoyment.
Photographs by A-Design by Gustavo Arredondo

Bradshaw Designs
Artful renovations translate to an improved home.

At its core, the kitchen is a room that facilitates meal preparation. But the discerning designers at Bradshaw Designs deliver spaces serving up a multitude of tasks—each as unique as its clients, who define how the heart of the home should beat. Julie Bradshaw, principal designer and founder of Bradshaw Designs, oversees each custom plan. The San Antonio-based firm prides itself on turnkey design, and remodeling. A creative, artful approach results in unique spaces, like one glass-themed reno Julie completed for a client who loved color and all things glass. Julie installed a glass-surfaced dining island that was recycled from razed office building windows. Another renovation resulted in a large, multi-functional pantry area. By the time the team was finished with it, the space featured an area for laundry and folding, gardening storage, and even computer space for online shopping and Pinterest perusing. It was finished off with a chic, sliding barn door that could conceal the area as desired. Innovative use of materials and textures allows Bradshaw Designs to successfully transform kitchens from utilitarian spaces into functional works of art.

LEFT: The 11-foot island and cooktop splash feature exquisite Calacatta marble. Gilded iron lanterns highlight gray-washed distressed beams on the soaring vaulted ceiling for a fresh updated feel.
Photograph by Jennifer Siu-Rivera

KITCHEN INSPIRATION

FAVORITE EXTRAVAGANT DESIGN FEATURES?
We love to add a beautiful slab of marble as a classic focal point. Unique lighting fixtures act as jewelry for a finishing touch of glam and sophistication.

MUST-HAVES?
Drawers, drawers, drawers with heavy duty, full-extension glides— sometimes soft-close. Our clients are surprised by how much more storage they have, even though their actual cabinet space may be reduced! We generally use natural stone countertops throughout our kitchens. Aside from the benefit of its inherent strength, marble is timeless.

ONE FEATURE YOU NEVER WANT TO SEE AGAIN?
Good riddance to large fluorescent light boxes! We've seen every intrusive, awkward shape imaginable!

A TREND YOU'RE IN LOVE WITH?
Open walls instead of wall cabinets, which leaves room for pretty wall sconces! And, may I add, this is only possible if there are ample drawers in your kitchen!

TOP & BOTTOM RIGHT: Original mosaic flooring was a treasure not taken lightly in this Monte Vista kitchen remodel. The gold and white mosaic tile, meticulously preserved during demolition, inspired touches of brushed brass in the lighting, hardware, vent hood, and even wire grilles. Calacatta gold marble, walnut wood counters, and handmade white subway tile feel fresh and updated with a nod to the past.

FACING PAGE: A beloved antique armoire inspired this uniquely handcrafted walnut refrigeration showpiece concealing a Sub-Zero integrated refrigerator. Taj Mahal Quartzite adds a luxurious touch to the island countertop.
Photographs by Jennifer Siu-Rivera

Casey Roy Design
Enthusiastic, bold design shows a zest for life.

There's not much that excites Casey Roy more than a good textile or an exciting pattern in vibrant colors. The outgoing, charismatic interior designer thrives on creating, be it decorating a new home from scratch or assisting clients with a hefty makeover to breathe new life into their living space. Kitchens are no exception, thanks to Casey's creative ability to infuse statement design but in a way that's easily navigated and lifestyle-friendly. It's this energetic affection for her industry that keeps the Dallas native and Texas A&M grad at the top of her game—and in high demand. In fact, clients need only get a look at her fashionably decked out office space, peppered with brightly colored accessories and smartly sourced statement furniture, to know that Casey has what it takes to produce unique, well thought out design. She honed her skills with various firms in North Carolina, Dallas, and San Antonio before establishing her namesake company, Casey Roy Design. She originally operated out of her two-bedroom bungalow yet the business grew quickly and she was soon able to expand. From Hill Country contemporary estates to city-style escapes and coastal-themed retreats, Casey and her team deliver remarkable interiors that inspire.

LEFT: The striking combination of materials establishes an aesthetic of refinement and a tone of welcome.
Photograph by Casey Dunn

KITCHEN INSPIRATION

EVERY KITCHEN DESIGN MUST INCLUDE?
It needs to include plenty of cabinet space customized for the way the homeowners use their kitchen, have a "wow" factor, and reflect the style and personality of the people who will enjoy using it.

MOST TIMELESS STYLE?
It's possible to design a timeless space in any style. The secret is keeping the palette of materials clean, intentional, and true to the architectural style.

BEST PLACE TO SPLURGE?
Focus on accentuating the most prominent feature of your kitchen—your eye will naturally go there, so make it fabulous. It may be the backsplash, range hood elevation, island countertop, unique cabinetry finishes, or configuration.

TOP RIGHT & BOTTOM RIGHT: Strong lines and distilled compositions define the dining room and kitchen of the coastal contemporary vacation home.

FACING PAGE: The dining area focuses on stunning ocean views and is adorned with hues of the beach below. Dramatic pops of color in the homeowner's contemporary art make a stylish statement.
Photographs by Matthew Niemann

CROSS

Honest craftsmanship equals seamless composition.

It's quite likely that Craig Scott's favorite day of the week is Monday. For many, that signifies the start of a dreaded workweek, but for Craig it means a fresh start loaded with possibility, thanks to his passion for craftsmanship. At CROSS, his full-service residential remodeling and custom home building company, clients are treated like royalty and structure is the backbone that seems to hold Craig's entire operation together. It comes as no surprise, really, since the valuable characteristic stems from his military background—he served in the Air Force—and motivated his entrepreneurial spirit when he decided to create his own business doing what he loves. It also ensures top-notch spaces that are designed to make an impact. CROSS touts plenty of in-house professionals that command skills from tile and sheetrock to carpentry and painting, meaning clients interact with trustworthy, skilled experts versus a variety of subcontractors. Luxury kitchens are undoubtedly one of the firm's specialties, evident by designs that feature natural stone or wood flooring, impressive custom cabinets, some enviable oversized islands and more. Credit it to Craig's love of Mondays and his dedicated drive to produce an impeccable project every time.

LEFT: The contrasting ornate kitchen island has harmonious elements.
Splendid artisan work is featured throughout.
Photograph courtesy of Cross

KITCHEN INSPIRATION

MOST SURPRISING DESIGN?
None of the designs surprise me. Every kitchen has its own character. Every house has a story. Every client has a memory. The professional designers that we work with really do a fabulous job of bringing every client's hopes and dreams to reality.

MOST UNUSUAL REQUEST?
Dog food drawer with an automatic water dispenser below.

CREATIVE WAYS TO CUSTOMIZE A KITCHEN?
Custom-cut stone backsplashes or one-of-a-kind tile backsplashes; varied heights of the countertops; a mixture of stone and wood counters like black walnut butcher block.

BEST PLACES TO SOURCE UNIQUE ITEMS?
The internet is a great resource, but sometimes it is hard to tell if the items are good quality. There's nothing better than the high-end distributors and very knowledgeable sales representatives who receive training by the factory representatives.

TOP RIGHT: The well balanced design incorporates a custom copper vent-a-hood, walnut cabinetry, farm house sink, and a dimensional stone backsplash.

BOTTOM RIGHT: The beautiful dual-sided island includes a vegetable sink and oversize drawer storage. Custom lighting was assembled and installed with expertise, for a flawless look.

FACING PAGE: The luxurious butler's pantry with custom cabinetry exhibits excellence in craftsmanship. The spacious design balances organizational needs with easy access.
Photographs courtesy of Cross

Dado Group

Spaces that contribute to the common good are the most beautiful.

Driven by a passion to creatively form elements into stunning structures, Kristin Wiese Hefty has long been inspired by the true art and beauty of architecture—from the bend in a raw steel staircase to the way a roof structure tucks into a canopy of mature red oaks. Equally important to her is building sustainable structures while adhering to principles that contribute to the greater good of society. She is able to do both at Dado Group, her San Antonio-based firm that provides mindful architectural design and construction services under one roof. Differentiated from many design-build companies, Dado Group maintains a unique approach as an architect-led design-build firm. Its design-centered work is grounded in a love for the natural materials and simple lines that express the building traditions of the region yielding comfortable, appropriate, and purposeful structures. Led by licensed architects, the experienced team seamlessly guides projects from concept to completion with efficiency, creativity, and continuity. Working in residential and commercial realms, Dado Group is collectively energized by positively impacting the community, as people move through, experience, and enjoy the striking spaces they have designed.

LEFT: With room for entertaining, the white macaubas quartzite island's surface is a contemporary complement to the kitchen's stainless steel countertops and integral stainless steel sink and backsplash. Floating shelves of eight-inch hickory, also used for flooring, flank either side of the sink.
Photograph by Mark Menjivar

LEFT: A glass enclosed entryway with raw steel staircase spans the home's two levels affording views of the outdoor screened dining porch. The use of low-e (low emissivity) glass in the stairwell and throughout the house insulates without sacrificing natural light. Heavy timbered overhangs protect from scorching South Texas sun.
Photograph by Mark Menjivar

BOTTOM LEFT: A cupola running the length of the dining/family room and operable casement windows bring balanced light and passive cooling into the home. Construction by David Mills Custom Homes.
Photograph by Mark Menjivar

BOTTOM RIGHT: Generous lower drawers provide ample storage, as dictated by the client's aversion to clutter. The quartzite backsplash complements the stainless steel cook surface and vent hood.
Photograph by Mark Menjivar

KITCHEN INSPIRATION

MOST ECONOMICAL WAY TO MAKE THE BIGGEST IMPACT?
Paint. It's truly amazing what a fresh coat of paint can do. If you want to go one step further, smooth out those orange peel textured walls first!

EVERY KITCHEN DESIGN MUST INCLUDE?
Natural light. It is so important in the kitchen, and I vote for windows instead of upper cabinets any day—within reason, of course! Dishes and glasses can generally be sorted in under-counter drawers.

CREATIVE WAYS TO CUSTOMIZE A KITCHEN?
I like using lots of under-counter storage in order to allow for the most open space above the countertop. Not only does this leave room above for windows, but it really opens up the space.

LEFT: A cantilevered white marble island holds an under-mount sink with a satin nickel goose neck faucet giving ample area for culinary creativity and for guests to mingle with the chef.

ABOVE: Clerestory windows infusing the kitchen with natural light allow full-height cabinets painted in Benjamin Moore's Black Iron to wrap around the open kitchen and dining spaces.
Photographs by Mark Menjivar

Lake | Flato Architects

Sustainability and design are two sides of the same coin.

The design professionals at Lake | Flato Architects respond to every project, whether rural or urban, traditional or contemporary, with one purpose: to make the home intrinsically rise up from its place, acknowledging the geographic, historical, and cultural context surrounding it. They believe that the details of the design will then naturally lead to healthy, enjoyable, and sustainable residences. As the specifics of the home emerge during the design process, various topics are addressed to help inform the final design, such as the intended use of the rooms, technologies that enhance practicality, and regional materials that link the home to its surroundings. Lake | Flato's collaborative studio environment certainly facilitates this concept as each person's passions and talents are utilized in many capacities. Inspired by both old and new architecture, the team expresses beauty not by a particular style or era, but rather by buildings that are responsive to the environment and inherently timeless.

LEFT: The kitchen, with its floating steel shelves, has a seamless connection with both the living area and the master bedroom loft above. The custom dining table was made from a fallen pecan tree found on-site after a heavy storm.
Photograph by Casey Dunn

KITCHEN INSPIRATION

MOST IMPORTANT ELEMENT OF KITCHEN DESIGN?
It depends on the family and how the space will be enjoyed. Sometimes form comes first, other times it's all about function. Naturally, it's ideal when the two meet somewhere in the middle.

TIPS TO KEEP A KITCHEN TIMELESS?
Go with natural materials of the highest quality. Even if your tastes change, you'll always love the original design.

KEY CONSIDERATIONS FOR A RENOVATION?
The best designs come to life when the architect, interior designer, and builder are involved from the very beginning. Well-organized collaboration yields the best results.

TOP RIGHT, BOTTOM RIGHT, & FACING PAGE: The simple, open-air living room pavilion is sheltered behind thick limestone walls that house a full working kitchen. Folding, slatted wood doors screen the private bath and storage areas.
Photographs by Casey Dunn

Lori Caldwell Designs

Home interiors reveal taste, lifestyle, and individuality.

For Lori Caldwell, spaces shouldn't reflect any one specific time or style. Timelessness inevitably results from keen design choices and personalized selections of furniture, art, and lighting. At her namesake firm, Lori and her team hone in on wants, needs, and elements that enhance the family's life, both aesthetically and functionally. It has to be beautiful but it also has to work; it's an art form that must be as practical as it is eye-catching. Although it's no easy task, Lori has perfected this delicate balance. Situated in San Antonio, Lori Caldwell Designs assists homeowners with an array of interior home needs. The team works with builders and architects to perfect the details of a space—from flooring materials and cabinetry to paint colors and backsplash designs. Nothing is out of their realm. They will also assist with any purchasing needs that may arise, a benefit that gives homeowners access to trade prices and selections they won't find anywhere else. Any type of home consultation is welcome with Lori and her crew; they will faithfully guide homeowners through any design needs.

TOP LEFT: Floating stairs and glass rails allow those who enter the home to see on into this sophisticated living area.

BOTTOM LEFT: From the outside looking in, this outdoor living space brings the beauty of the indoors outside and provides a wonderful place for friends and family to gather.

FACING PAGE: The beautifully composed kitchen has bold colors and organic lines.
Photographs by Matthew Niemann

M Interiors

Boldly mixed styles make for colorfully comfortable living.

When it comes to interior design, Melissa Morgan is never one to shy away from making a statement and mixing materials. Perhaps it's her decade-long career in corporate law, her unfettered passion for creating beautiful spaces, or her San Antonio-based design business, M Interiors, that's garnered attention near and far. She also draws a great deal of inspiration from her travels, especially France. It could well be the latter—she admittedly loves spending time in Paris—that inspires her penchant for vintage furniture pieces and striking accessories. Her kitchen designs, for instance, have ranged from neutral-toned clean-lined spaces touting cream cabinets, marble flooring, oversized islands set with non-traditional bar stools—think bamboo-style—and statement light fixtures to a cozy breakfast nook with a dark wood table, airy windows for lots of natural light, and a rustic buffet with a large mirror and colorful porcelain plates hanging above it on the wall. It's spaces like these that prove the designer thrives on skillfully pulling together looks that reflect the owner's lifestyle and personality, even meshing a variety of styles into one space.

LEFT: The light-filled dining room includes a late Georgian dining table, an 18th-century inlaid sideboard, and a pair of Louis XVI demi-lune tables. Also adding to the room's warmth are hand-painted French panels and a sparkling antique crystal chandelier.
Photograph by Mark Menjivar

KITCHEN INSPIRATION

BEST ADVICE?
Don't build a kitchen for the dinners you may throw once a year. Build a kitchen that suits your family's needs.

TIMELESS OR TRENDY?
Definitely timeless. Kitchens are too much of an investment to have something go out of style!

FAVORITE ASPECT OF YOUR OWN KITCHEN?
Simplicity of materials—stainless steel counters and a wonderful built-in stone breakfast table original to the mid-century house.

ONE EXTRAVAGANT DESIGN FEATURE?
A really fantastic espresso machine.

TOP LEFT: A large and varied collection of Chinese Famille Rose porcelain adorn the grasspaper-covered walls of this breakfast room. Also included are an antique marble demi-lune and a custom antique porcelain lamp.

BOTTOM LEFT: Pink silk velvet Louis XVI dining chairs pop in the sky-high retreat. The dining area also includes a custom Italian Lucite and glass dining table and a vintage white glass credenza.

FACING PAGE: Bright and open, the kitchen is perfect for entertaining a large crowd or just family. The French bistro barstools and custom light fixture complete the functional yet beautiful space.
Photographs by Mark Menjivar

Overland Partners

Architecture is about creating a unique reflection of people.

Some of history's greatest architects designed in both the commercial and residential realms, and the team at Overland Partners is no exception. Renowned for spectacular museums and visitors' centers, the firm also creates a handful of residences each year. So how do high-profile public works projects translate to private residences? Perhaps the residences are best described as private museums. Many of the firm's clients have specialized interests, and those interests are wonderful inspiration for the design of their homes. The Overland team often integrates fine art and other collections into the architecture, articulating people's unique life stories to create meaningful spaces. Overland Partners takes a highly collaborative approach to design, so the homeowners are involved at every step, and their personality and preferences are woven into every aspect of the design. Many of the firm's residential clients commission the firm after memorable experiences working on institutional projects. Impressed at the strict adherence to deadlines and budgets, level of personal interaction, and of course the designs themselves, these homeowners appreciate that the essentials of creating exceptional architecture span every project type and style.

LEFT: With a collection of more than 100 masterworks of postwar paintings, sculptures, and works on paper, the clients desired a home that would not only complement their collection but allow them to experience art in their daily lives.
Photograph by James F. Wilson

TOP LEFT & TOP RIGHT: Odyssey, a 1936 cottage in Carmel-by-the-Sea, is reinterpreted for a 21st-century progressive sensibility. The interior's teak is free of screws, nails, and visible fasteners of any kind, demonstrating how rustic timber and stone can be expressed with jewel box refinement. The new dual-corridor design features an open-plan kitchen at the center.
Photographs by John Edward Linden

LEFT: Light coves that conceal LED, linear fluorescent, and track lighting fixtures change the quality and quantity of light during the day to mimic the color and intensity of natural light. This allows for museum-quality lighting levels in certain conditions, as well as warm, intimate residential lighting levels.
Photograph by James F. Wilson

FACING PAGE: Befitting the high desert terrain, the lower half of the residence is buried into a hillside, its low profile further emphasized by a series of landscaped roofs. Fully integrating the structure with the site, the house wraps around the crest of a hill on three sides, creating framed views of the landscape in all directions.
Photograph by Robert Reck

KITCHEN INSPIRATION

WHAT'S RESPONSIVE DESIGN?
Design that is specific to the owner and the site. A kitchen's flow, for instance, needs to reflect how the family lives. The space should be oriented to take in the views. The palette of materials should respond to the local vernacular.

MUST-HAVES?
There should always be a convenient, comfortable place for others to help, sit, visit, and eat together.

HOW LARGE SHOULD A KITCHEN BE?
Kitchens need to work on many levels, functionally and aesthetically, so they should be spacious enough to fulfill all of these requirements. They should be treated as extended living rooms that are open and welcoming so that people enjoy lingering together.

TOP RIGHT & BOTTOM RIGHT: The house provides direct access to the water and is concealed from the neighboring residential development by a stone landscape wall. Four dominant building materials—concrete, sandstone, steel, and glass—are utilized throughout the home; they were chosen as much for their local availability as for their differing textures and distinct characteristics. The repeated use of stone and concrete in both interior and exterior applications further dissolves the boundaries between indoors and out.

FACING PAGE: Set along the water's edge in Horseshoe Bay, Texas, the residence consists of three concrete pavilions connected by a courtyard, maintaining a strong connection with the outdoors throughout the home.
Photographs by Paul Bardagjy

Palmer Todd

The kitchen will always be the heart of the home.

In these modern times, the kitchen is more than a place where people cook. It's a place where people live. The designers at Palmer Todd understand that and enjoy making the kitchen of a home a place that fully expresses the family who lives in it. By taking into account the use of space in addition to the family's personality and vision, Palmer Todd creates spaces that work. Listening carefully to the desires of the client allows the design team at Palmer Todd to separate the tangible from the intangible, arranging thoughts that result in dream kitchens. Here, great design and great products work hand-in-hand, as reputable vendors are considered part of the design team. Kitchens are more than a standard assembly of cabinets, tile, countertops, and appliances. They are artful compositions and expressions of the people who live in them. These guiding principles flow through the firm's kitchen designs into other areas of the home, rendering consistently solid design.

LEFT: A focal point of the home, the kitchen utilizes symmetry as a design statement as well as an organizing element.
Photograph by Tre Dunham

TOP LEFT & BOTTOM LEFT: The fully remodeled mid-century modern home has a fresh, contemporary aesthetic while respecting the original architecture.

ABOVE: The lake house's outdoor entertaining area was designed for fun.

FACING PAGE: Unusual and eclectic yet functional, the materials establish a hospitable ambience in the kitchen designed for serious cooking and frequent entertaining.
Photographs by Casey Dunn

TOP LEFT: Whimsical touches define the modern lakefront home.
Photograph by Casey Dunn

TOP RIGHT: The kitchen embodies classic elegance with an Atlanta feel.
Photograph by Casey Dunn

BOTTOM LEFT: Stylish and functional, the ranch-style home's kitchen area comfortably accommodates a dozen dinner guests.
Photograph by Tre Dunham

FACING PAGE: The homeowner requested a modern space with a dramatic focal point, which the design delivers in spades.
Photographs by Casey Dunn

PREVIOUS PAGES: The completely renovated King William historical home elegantly mixes old and new while blending in an industrial flair.
Photographs by Casey Dunn

KITCHEN INSPIRATION

BEST WAY TO BEGIN A REDESIGN?
We typically start by asking our clients what it is that they are most unhappy with in their current space. We then follow that up with an extensive interview on their lifestyle. How do they like to cook and how many cooks are there? Do they like to entertain? Do they have children? If so, what are their ages? Asking these questions helps us to better understand their needs so we can provide a space that is not only beautiful but also functions well.

MOST ECONOMICAL WAY TO MAKE THE BIGGEST IMPACT?
A unique backsplash or a fun lighting element.

PERSPECTIVE ON DIFFERENT WAYS KITCHENS NEED TO FUNCTION?
We tend to think of the functionality of a space in terms of zones. Every part of a kitchen is designed to serve a particular function. We have now separated those activities based on the families that engage in them, and we have created separate spaces where they can occur. For example, there would be prep zones, baking zones, specialty zones—like a desk or a designated area for children's homework or artwork—clean-up area, and so on.

Symmetry Architects, page 225

L. Lumpkins, Architect, page 209

Calais Custom Homes, page 163

DALLAS / FT. WORTH

AG Builders Custom Homes

Every project tells a story, every detail has a purpose.

AG Builders comprises a group of talented artisans who operate under the direction of Gary and Lisa Nussbaum. A third-generation master craftsman hailing from the Midwest, Gary passionately carries on the family legacy, approaching projects with a stellar combination of classical craftsmanship and cutting-edge construction methods. Lisa's unique background—bachelor's degrees in interior designer and psychology as well as a master's and a PhD in psychology, earned locally at UNT with studies abroad at Oxford and Cambridge—make her particularly adept at translating people's dreams for their new homes into buildable plans. Good design and superior craftsmanship supersede trends. AG Builders believes that a good structure is needed at the core of every project. The events of life cause individuals and families to grow and change. Interior design makes an enormous contribution to space and is the key to turning a house into a home.

TOP LEFT: The dining room is anchored by the butler's pantry and wine bar area, which features backlit black cloud onyx that creates a romantic and alluring ambience for evening entertaining.

BOTTOM LEFT & FACING PAGE: Luxurious materials, textures, and colors create a sense of sophisticated elegance. French eclectic in style, the space utilizes symmetry as an organizing element and asymmetry for a dash of the unexpected. The black soapstone granite, fumo di londra granite as the main island, painted ceiling, gray-washed cabinets, and baroque tile backsplash play wonderful counterpoint to one another. A well-planned palette of creams and grays fosters a sense of elegance. The kitchen features statement-making light fixtures, stainless steel appliances, and brushed nickel faucets, all from Ferguson Enterprises.
Photographs by Michael Gilbreath

KITCHEN INSPIRATION

MOST EXTRAVAGANT WAY TO SET THE STYLE?
We love to work with gorgeous range/oven/vent hood combinations by the likes of La Cornue and Lacanche. This is where most of our kitchen designs start because it makes such a solid statement.

UNIQUELY CUSTOMIZED KITCHENS?
For a very independent older couple, we created a stylish, user-friendly kitchen with counter height and faucet placement perfectly tailored to their needs. Another couple enjoys side-by-side islands, each with its own sink, so there's plenty of workspace while preparing meals—and they lived happily ever after.

THINGS TO ENSURE?
Electrical plugs are not visible in the backsplash, there is plenty of counter space, and floorplans have a proper place to gather and entertain.

RECOMMENDATIONS FOR GOING IT ALONE?
Don't do it. You'll appreciate working with a good designer who will assess your needs, consider your preferred style, and value engineer the design to work with your budget and give you the kitchen of your dreams.

LEFT & FACING PAGE: The breathtaking aesthetic is the result of intense collaboration between the design team and the homeowners. Designed expressly for the needs and wishes of the busy couple, the kitchen includes a coffee bar, storage solutions that make the space easy to maintain, and a flow that is efficient without sacrificing an ounce of style. A decided focal point, the island is curved to lend an organic, softer feel to the otherwise rectilinear space; the suspended working surface offers dramatic appeal. Gray stained floors give the home an industrial chic appeal, and stainless steel appliances furnished by Ferguson Enterprises provide a desirable contrast to the black lacquer cabinets milled by Gary Nussbaum.
Photographs by Michael Gilbreath

ArTex Development
Every design has its own unique character and personality.

Precise attention to detail meets 21st century design and construction at ArTex Development, a boutique firm specializing in both custom builds and residential renovations. Principals Mitch Lee, Randall Oxford, and Ross Boorhem treat each and every project as if it were their own, skillfully managing the process from concept to completion as they turn their clients' architectural and design dreams from basic sketch into reality. The interesting thing about the ArTex group is that they have also successfully renovated a multitude of their own investment properties for resale in addition to working with many homeowners to do the same. They are acutely aware of the many intricacies and challenges of a renovation project and provide expert guidance to ensure a high-quality, budget-minded result that only exceeds expectations. Realizing that any design venture is an important commitment, ArTex has built its reputation on being a sound investment. From its team of award-winning architects and high-profile designers to their detail-oriented supervision, the firm distinguishes itself with a significant level of talent and service.

LEFT: Embracing the open floor plan of this downtown Dallas loft, a custom steel table features hand-finished walnut harvested from the client's family farm in Alabama. The adjacent dry bar and floating shelves are tight-grained white oak.
Photograph by Sean McGinty

KITCHEN INSPIRATION

BEST WAY TO BEGIN A REDESIGN?

Research must happen before a redesign. We invest a significant amount of time in understanding clients' design tastes and preferences while learning how they actually live day to day. Visual references and examples are also imperative to jumpstart the creative process—from architectural magazines and design websites to other visual references including our previously completed projects. We always encourage clients to keep an open mind; outside-the-box ideas frequently result in the most exciting features of a completed home.

PERSPECTIVE ON DIFFERENT WAYS KITCHENS NEED TO FUNCTION?

The design and functionality of a kitchen should be as individual as the personality of the owners and should reflect their lifestyle—from the non-cook who wants a showpiece kitchen yet only uses the refrigerator and microwave to the constant baker who is always entertaining family and friends.

MOST ECONOMICAL WAY TO MAKE THE BIGGEST IMPACT?

A sleek, clean backsplash creates a world of difference and can easily be achieved by relocating outlets and switch plates from the backsplash to under the upper cabinets. Also, clutter-free countertops that are free of appliances and other utilitarian objects make a strong statement—relocate those items to an appliance garage or pantry!

TOP RIGHT: A wine column commands center stage in this dramatic expansion of a home that was once served as the Texas Christian University chancellor's home.
Photograph by Brandon Colston

BOTTOM RIGHT: Creating an open-concept kitchen for amateur-chef clients meant creating ample seating for entertaining while cooking.
Photograph by Leah Biemacki

FACING PAGE: An outdoor mechanical room and porch were incorporated into a small existing kitchen to modernize a century-old Dallas estate property.
Photograph by Sean McGinty

Bella Vita Custom Homes

A home's aesthetic is a reflection of the soul.

Custom homebuilding is truly an art for the talented professionals at Bella Vita Custom Homes. With Andy Clem at the helm, Bella Vita delivers bespoke detail-oriented homes that are not only energy-efficient but also impeccably designed. A diverse team of professionals is hand-selected—including top subcontractors, suppliers, AIA architects, ASID interior designers, and more— to ensure that each home is built with great skill and quality materials. They work closely with homeowners in understanding and participating with each phase of the creative process, from new home builds to extensive kitchen renovations. An inspiration photo is often the starting point for the team's makeovers, as it helps to identify the kitchen components that are most appealing—ample counter space, additional storage, a large island or two, and top-grade appliances. The culmination of such a coordinated approach to planning, design, construction, and final touches results in ecstatic homeowners and spaces that are both functional and beautiful.

LEFT: From two-step crown molding and the decorative eight-inch box beam ceiling treatments to the white oak rifts and quartered floors, the kitchen is beautifully detailed from top to bottom.
Photograph courtesy of Bella Vita Custom Homes

KITCHEN INSPIRATION

THOUGHTS ON REFINISHING VERSUS REPLACING?
Refinishing is ideal to restore an element within your kitchen, whereas replacement is ideal for establishing a completely new look or feel. Typically, the cost to replace is not a lot more than re-facing. Re-facing is much faster but you are very limited in making substantial improvements to functionality.

BEST PLACES TO SOURCE UNIQUE ITEMS?
Dallas is overflowing with amazing home design showrooms and stores. Whether you're building a new home or updating your current home, we recommend traveling to the Dallas Design District to find tile at Ann Sacks, antiques at Dolly Python Vintage, Flor for carpet tiles, and Stash Designs for unique, upcycled items.

WHAT MAKES KITCHENS DREAMY?
Thoughtful layouts and spacious floor plans that include expansive islands, top-grade appliances, exquisitely detailed custom cabinets, ample lighting, high level of detail and architectural elements. All of these elements elevate the space into the highest echelons of kitchen design.

TOP RIGHT: Every kitchen design must take to heart the maxim of having a place for everything, and having everything in its place. This cutting board drawer is located directly over a pullout trash container to ensure waste is instantly and cleanly disposed of. Whereas the spice cabinet doubles as a hidden door which opens to the expansive walk-in pantry. Completed with twin dishwashers and Wolf appliances, this kitchen is a chef's dream!

BOTTOM RIGHT: This gourmet kitchen at Bella Vita's Preston Hollow model home provides ample storage with open counter space to allow hosts to prepare delicious meals while simultaneously entertaining their guests.

FACING PAGE: Aside from the granite countertops, eggshell finish cabinets, and red oak nail down wood floors, these ET2 contemporary lights from the Larmes Collection really tie this contemporary kitchen together.
Photographs courtesy of Bella Vita Custom Homes

Berry Marble and Granite

Every design element is a chance to make a bold statement.

Ask owner Craig Berry of Berry Marble and Granite what makes his company different from the competition and you'll get an answer with no hesitation: it's the people. Approachable, informed, and prepared for anything, the experts at Berry Marble and Granite encourage tough questions and creative thinking from homeowners, builders, and contractors alike. Working in Texas since the early 1990s, Craig knows what residents want and has kept up with trends in technology, using the most advanced equipment imported directly from Italy. Promising not only efficiency and accuracy, Craig knows that his all-digital, computer-based system offers homeowners and builders peace of mind. Previews of specific selections can be seen before the installation begins. Imagine seeing a marble vanity, hand-crafted stone detailing, and a sparkling new shower in your bathroom prior to making the long-term commitment. Located in Tyler, the extensive showroom line-up features cultured marble, granite, and natural stone, with patterns and tones that bring bathtubs, countertops, and interior accessories to life.

TOP LEFT & FACING PAGE: The waterfall-edge island in Calcutta Gold is beautifully paired with absolute black granite countertops with a leather finish.

BOTTOM LEFT: Multicolored Pakistani Onyx figures prominently in the master bath.
Photographs by Danny Piassick

Bottega Design Gallery

Artists can tell stories without saying a word.

Named for an Italian-style artist's studio or creative workshop, Bottega Design Gallery is the product of Rebecca Farris' desire to bring high style and beautiful craftsmanship to the American design scene. Forever inspired by her interior design studies abroad, the tile and stone maven believes that her company's creative medium is more than an aesthetic. The perfect tile and stone tell the story of a home and its family. Bottega offers an artistic selection of products, from backsplash mosaics, walls, and flooring to mantelpieces, all made with materials of the finest quality. If you don't know the difference between ceramic and clay tiles, how to best utilize waterjet tiles, or even where to begin when considering all the options, Bottega is a welcoming place of learning. The designers are more than happy to walk clients through the basics or provide comprehensive design recommendations to ensure that the selections are space-appropriate and timelessly incorporated.

TOP: Custom black and white terracotta tiles with an exposed terracotta edge tie together the timeless brass details found throughout the space.

BOTTOM: Handcrafted and elegant, the custom charcoal and grey concrete tile makes a bold, one-of-a-kind statement.

FACING PAGE: The laser-cut, etched stone backsplash blends the kitchen's classic details and vintage charm.
Photographs by Shoot2Sell

Calais Custom Homes

Your home is a reflection of your persona.

Limiting the number of clients you work with in a calendar year seems to defy the traditional laws of business. But Todd Handwerk says the explanation is simple: quality. He and his senior team have an amazingly hand-on approach, and they ensure that all of their projects live up to the Calais Custom Homes reputation by accepting only as many commissions as they can personally oversee. Sharing its name with an elegant French seaside town steeped in history and aesthetic perfection, the company builds homes in the full spectrum of architectural vernaculars, from classical to contemporary. While some styles call for specific building techniques, the focus on creating homes of enduring quality is a constant. The unusually generous warranty program bears testament to the level of home the company builds. Calais residences dot the North Texas landscape, some taking advantage of easy access to downtown attractions, others enjoying the prestige of the area's most posh neighborhoods. Because the location, style, and atmosphere of a home speak volumes about the people who live there, the Calais team takes particular care when teaming up with architects and other design professionals to ensure that the home not only suits the residents' lifestyle but echoes their values, tastes, and social status.

LEFT: Beautiful craftsmanship and detailing abound in the timeless, transitional-style kitchen of a Highland Park home.
Photograph by Danny Piassick

KITCHEN INSPIRATION

THOUGHTS ON KITCHEN CONSTRUCTION?
The more open, the better. Whether you like to entertain or just be connected as a family while making dinner, you can't go wrong with a wide open layout.

TOP THINGS TO AVOID?
We always advocate timeless design for built-in elements. If you want to do something unexpected, have fun with decorative accents or wall colors, things that can be changed easily.

AN INTERESTING KITCHEN TREND?
Kitchens have become so open that we are seeing an increased desire for secondary kitchen spaces—catering areas, sculleries, back kitchens, prep kitchens.

TOP RIGHT: The Highland Park catering kitchen demonstrates that gray is the new beige. Custom millwork, stainless steel appliances, and stone flooring uniquely laid in the herringbone pattern are punctuated by the eye-catching backsplash.

BOTTOM RIGHT: The dark cabinetry, light stone counters, and warmly stained floors establish a contemporary vibe in the Chateau du Lac home.

FACING PAGE: Embodying all that is wonderful about French country style, the kitchen of a Vaquero home features distressed beams, masonry walls, and fine cabinetry with a collected look. Double islands make food preparation and entertaining a breeze.
Photographs by Danny Piassick

Clarke And Doyle Living
A home is meant to be loved.

Clarke And Doyle is an interior design firm that started in 2013 to provide a fresh start for North Texas style and an equally fresh start for its owner, Cynthia Doyle. For 30 years Cynthia was a stay-at-home mom, designing for her friends and family before finally accepting the persistent, loving push from relatives to share her talent with the public. These humble beginnings have given Cynthia a practical approach to design and a disarmingly earnest personality that makes her a trusted confidant. The residents of Arlington, where Clarke And Doyle is located, quickly discovered that her style is as approachable as she is, while in no way lacking in sophistication. Under Cynthia's attentive watch, Clarke And Doyle has made it easy for people to have a fashion-forward, polished look that fits their lifestyle, all the while reinventing a timeless style that is easy to love.

TOP LEFT: A subdued color palette makes the kitchen feel spacious and soothing. A touch of greenery and warm wood floors complement the palette and bring life to its cool hues.

BOTTOM LEFT: The round table creates an easy flow to the room while also allowing extra space for dramatic pieces like the modern bookcase turned china cabinet. All furniture provided by Clarke And Doyle Living.

FACING PAGE: The double islands provide abundant workspace along with a perfect setup for entertaining. The spacious outer island makes for an ideal serving station and gathering place.
Photographs courtesy of Clarke And Doyle Living

CMI Designs | Quatre C's, LLC

Create a design that induces ease and beauty aligning function with style.

Carol Carpenter has always had an eye for design. As the former head of sales for a Dallas-based fashion company, Carol transitioned quite naturally into interior design. Her craft grew organically over the course of 25 years as homeowners returned to her again and again, not only to design, but this time to remodel their homes. When a client asked her to build a home from the ground up, Carol's role and passion as a builder was solidified. Today, Carol is the owner of two companies: Quatre C's, LLC, her construction business, and CMI Designs, her interior design firm. Her unique perspective on home building originates from her understanding of both construction and design, coupled with the keen ability to meld the two into a beautiful, comfortable space. She attends every meeting between the homeowner and the architect, paying attention to every detail, and isn't shy about changing construction plans to better serve the overall design. Carol's innate sense of space, color, and light helps develop well-conceived floor plans that accommodate flow. She excels in incorporating the homeowner's style, while enhancing it with her personal vision. She believes a home should look acquired by incorporating family favorites, and at the same time look like it was just updated. With her finger on the pulse of the latest trends, Carol always encourages homeowners to explore new designs and styles.

LEFT: The waterfall stone counters add the perfect amount of drama to the otherwise calm palette of materials. Clean lines in the open layout are complemented by strategic pops of color to foster a contemporary vibe.
Photograph by Danny Piassick

KITCHEN INSPIRATION

WHAT'S SOMETHING EVERY KITCHEN DESIGN SHOULD INCLUDE?
A great kitchen design gives its users a feeling of beauty and makes their daily tasks easier to accomplish. In order to create a design for a client, I always ask three questions when looking at their kitchen: What do you like? What don't you like? What would you do differently? Doing a full-scale analysis of what's currently in their kitchen and how they would change it helps develop a custom design. Obviously, you're supposed to have the "triangle," of your sink, refrigerator, and cooktop, but there are no hard and fast rules about where you put them. My kitchen designs have "inner beauty" as well because I think about the insides of the cabinets and how they should be customized to fit my clients' needs.

WHAT'S IN YOUR DREAM KITCHEN?
I personally don't like a lot of clutter, especially in the kitchen. I like to maximize storage by using floor-to-ceiling cabinets. This creates a very clean look, which allows you to have your small appliances and designated areas of use behind pocket doors. Where I have countertops, I want open space above: either minimal or no cabinetry, or maybe just a few open shelves. I like having a wall for the backsplash to go from countertop to the ceiling, creating a dramatic visual behind the sink or cooktop. Dual sinks and dishwashers are a must and I would have two single ovens, both at countertop height. My dream kitchen would have customized cabinets to fit my needs and have the latest and greatest technology in appliances and fixtures, including all the fabulous cooking gadgets that have come out on the market. Lastly, my kitchen would be located in the house where you can have the best view of the outdoors.

TOP RIGHT: Outdoor kitchens deserve to be just as functional and beautiful as their indoor counterparts.

BOTTOM RIGHT: Soft tones in the cabinetry, flooring, and counters draw attention to the natural landscape.

FACING PAGE TOP: The dark backsplash was a bold choice yet it perfectly anchors the composition.

FACING PAGE BOTTOM: While the aesthetic is classically beautiful, the kitchen was designed with practicality and entertaining foremost in mind.
Photographs by Danny Piassick

Couto Homes

When it's done well, you just know.

There's no shortage of homebuilders that will promise to build a beautiful home. Couto Homes builds beautiful homes and—even more impressively—makes the process fun. Couto Homes is a certified master builder, one of fewer than 50 in the entire state. That kind of recognition didn't happen overnight. It's the product of hard work, determination, and the relentless pursuit of perfection by the father-son team of Al and Donny Couto. Treating every project as if it were for their own family, they continue to fine-tune their processes with each home they build, occasionally learning the hard way how to do something even better but always doing whatever it takes to get the job done right. Al and Donny liken the homebuilding process to an invigorating puzzle that begins the moment clients reveal a vague wish list of what they think they want and how they think it might look. Of course, through a series of conversations and planning sessions, the Couto team turns this loose vision into a buildable plan where function and beauty are in perfect harmony. The space comes to life first through detailed three-dimensional renderings that give the future residents an understanding of scale, perspective, and lighting. Once the layout is perfected, the fixtures and finishes are carefully selected to ensure that the home's aesthetic matches the level of quality behind each wall.

LEFT: The homeowners sought a look they had only seen in magazines and online. After extensive thought and an abundance of collaborative work, the timeless design came together, offering aesthetic beauty and complete functionality.
Photograph by Matrix Tours

KITCHEN INSPIRATION

MOST ECONOMICAL WAY TO MAKE THE BIGGEST IMPACT?
Opt for simple layouts, and allocate the money you save on the eye candy: luxurious materials and fine fixtures.

HOW DOES A KITCHEN NEED TO FUNCTION?
A good design includes at least one good gathering spot and food prep areas that make the chef's job easy and fun. Kitchens are also important areas for homework and family projects, coming up with new recipes, and baking—don't underestimate how much space baking requires. These varied uses lend themselves to designs that are easy to clean and maintain.

TOP: Family and function meets transitional style. This kitchen proves wonderful for a family gathering and entertaining with an open concept, stunning lighting, inviting paint colors, great use of space and flow, and a modern feel to the overall design.

BOTTOM: The homeowner wanted a timeless design that would be beautiful and function as a space where family and friends gather.

FACING PAGE: A perfect expression of personality, the kitchen boasts rich colors and timeless class. From the floor to the ceiling every detail was well thought out and planned for this look. The space is perfect for so many reasons: function, design, entertaining, the love of cooking, and catching up on conversation with family and friends.
Photographs by Matrix Tours

DeLeo & Fletcher Design

Design is transformative.

Fran DeLeo and Mark Fletcher are the innovators behind DeLeo & Fletcher Design. They believe that the foundation of creating tailored spaces lies in fully understanding their clients' personal preferences, vision, and sense of style, while responding to the distinct attributes of the site, architecture, and locale. Their process is collaborative from beginning to end. Fran and Mark serve as liaisons for their clients, working as a team with the architect, builder, and homeowners through the entire design process to produce luxurious homes that suit the unique personalities and lifestyles of the residents. By lending their creative perspective at every step, they yield distinctive designs that are refreshingly distilled, thoughtfully developed, and delightfully one-of-a-kind.

LEFT: The kitchen is introduced with an antique beam that combines rustic, modern, and tailored materials. The inset arched window was custom made to highlight the beautiful backdrop of nature.
Photograph by Danny Piassick Photography

KITCHEN INSPIRATION

MOST ECONOMICAL WAY TO MAKE THE BIGGEST IMPACT?
Dramatic lighting fixtures can be a cost effective way to bring
personality and life to a kitchen.

EVERY KITCHEN DESIGN MUST INCLUDE?
Beautiful tile.

TRICKS OF THE TRADE?
We are mindful to incorporate plenty of hidden storage and organizers
so that everything has a place. This makes it easy to keep the counters
clear and the environment free of clutter so the kitchen is not only
beautiful, but also efficient.

ABOVE: Handmade tiles draw your eye to the playful bar area off the
dining room.

TOP RIGHT: Custom quatrefoil tiles with a peacock crackled glaze
complement the burnished pewter and pearl stone hood.

BOTTOM RIGHT: An artistic blend of waterfall crackled glass accentuates the
game room bar.

FACING PAGE: Accents of tangerine and soft blue-grays contrast with the
walnut, Mediterranean-inspired cabinetry for a fresh and fun palette.
Photographs by Danny Piassick Photography

Douglas Paul Designs
The beauty is in the details.

Douglas Horton's attention to execution and detail manifests itself in luxuriously elegant kitchens brimming with functionality and surprises. With every project, he takes his vision and implements it with the client's desires and needs. Meshing those ideas together creates more than pleasing environments that homeowners can enjoy on a daily basis for years to come. Working in a boutique firm atmosphere allows Douglas to pay attention to minute details while forming personal relationships that endure once the project is complete. Though his designs often involve complex concepts, the process is always enjoyable for all. For Douglas, the essence of a project involves creating and designing unique styles that express the clients' personality while attending to their needs. Homeowners should feel at home the minute they begin cooking dinner in their new space.

LEFT: The charm of the home is an understated formality with a sense of comfort and warmth that is inviting for family and entertaining.
Photographs by Terry Wier Photography

DW Design Group
Custom is always in style.

In the design world, change is the only constant. It's exciting, exhilarating—and also a bit intimidating. Just as fashion fads come and go, so too do interior design trends. Led by Dennis Waters, ASID, and Nick Nussrallah, Allied ASID, the professionals of DW Design Group are ever abreast of what's hot, what's on its way out, and what will look amazing in a decade or perhaps even a century from now. Sensitive to the unique requirements of each project, they know how to create environments that perfectly echo and enhance the residents' lifestyles. Some are most comfortable surrounded by classical design while others prefer a more contemporary feel. Regardless of the desired aesthetic, the DW Design Group team has a slew of resources for decorative materials and furnishings. Custom window treatments and rugs are somewhat of a specialty because the designers believe that these elements have tremendous power to unify the design and make a truly one-of-a-kind style statement. Whether focusing on the smallest of details for an installation or partnering with the architect to dream up a grand scheme, the designers take a collaborative approach to ensure that every plan is thoughtful, cohesive, and timeless.

LEFT: The spacious, Tuscan-inspired kitchen is ideal for family gatherings. Cabinetry in warm alder wood tones and custom designed tiles for the backsplash make a timeless and handsome statement. Builder: Dan Thomas Custom Homes. Architect: Schaumburg Architect Associates, AIA. *Photograph by Alan Glazener*

ABOVE: Visible from the foyer, the spectacular view of the swimming pool and cabana makes a wonderful first impression and a dramatic setting for the formal living room. The patterned floors are travertine and wood. The elegant furniture is from Tomlinson Erwin-Lambeth.

LEFT: The open floorplan fully integrates the great room, casual dining area, and kitchen. Hand-scraped wood floors, beams, natural stone fireplace, and leather seating foster an appealing warmth.

FACING PAGE: The stunning master bath embodies Romanesque style with travertine columns, a mosaic barrel ceiling, and a patterned travertine floor.
Photographs by Alan Glazener

KITCHEN INSPIRATION

CREATIVE WAYS TO CUSTOMIZE A KITCHEN?
Make full use of the space and let form follow function. If you like salads, create a salad station where everything is at your fingertips when it comes to preparation and plating.

THOUGHTS ON REFINISHING VERSUS REPLACING?
We use 20 years as a rubric for how long cabinets should last, though quality must be carefully examined before determining if it's best to replace or refinish. We often refinish cabinets that initially seem like they're ready to be replaced. A beautiful paint or stain—combined with new hinges, drawer glides, and decorative hardware—can breathe new life into cabinetry.

BEST PLACES TO GET IDEAS?
Model homes and showrooms are great places to familiarize yourself with the latest trends, though of course it's always beneficial to have a designer guide you through the maze of choices—in redesigns and new construction projects alike.

TOP RIGHT: The contemporary kitchen's cantilevered glass bar countertop is an exciting design element.

BOTTOM RIGHT: The sophisticated master bath represents the best of modern spa style.

FACING PAGE TOP LEFT: Spacious, light, and defined by handsome curving lines, the contemporary home is wonderfully unique.

FACING PAGE TOP RIGHT: Streamlined design and natural materials create a sense of warmth.

FACING PAGE BOTTOM LEFT: Induction cooking and a view of the living area bring the home to the pinnacle of modern living.

FACING PAGE BOTTOM RIGHT: Strong architectural features envelop the living space with a pleasing mixture of natural light and textures. The "ribbon" fireplace provides a focal point that is visible from the kitchen, dining areas, and living room. Home Builder: Dan Thomas Custom Homes. Architect: Schaumburg Architect Associates, AIA.
Photographs by David Lyles Photography

Gary Riggs Home
Timeless beauty is a daily treat.

An artist at heart, Gary Riggs brings intrinsic art principles into all of his interiors. Taking great care to consider color, line, texture, and balance, Gary, who has more than two decades of design experience, approaches every space as if it were a canvas awaiting magnificent brushstrokes. In creating a residence, he urges his clients to embrace the elements that are important to them as individuals and to also think about how they want to feel in the space. This creates a timeless beauty in a home that will give homeowners and their guests pleasure every day. With astounding attention to detail, Gary takes each project from concept to completion to ensure that expectations are always exceeded. Even though his designs are thoroughly planned and executed, the result is an effortless look that enhances the overall experience. His design process renders luxurious interiors featuring a variety of textures and finishes that welcome and comfort, as well as illustrate the personalities and tastes of his discerning clientele. And just like any true artist, Gary can't wait for the next canvas.

LEFT: Beautiful millwork furthers the connection between the kitchen and living spaces.
Photograph by Mark Herron Photography

TOP RIGHT, BOTTOM RIGHT, & FACING PAGE: Varied in style yet all possessing a high level of refinement, the dining rooms are informed by symmetry, soothing colors, and dramatic lighting.
Photographs by Mark Herron Photography

LEFT: The beamed ceiling complements the medium-toned flooring to accentuate the sense of spaciousness.

FACING PAGE: Rich textures and strategic pops of color lend a playful elegance to the living areas.
Photographs by Mark Herron Photography

KITCHEN INSPIRATION

BEST WAY TO BEGIN A REDESIGN?

Think about where you are in your life and what you want the space to achieve. If you're an empty nester, your kitchen can be more sophisticated and you might not even need as much space. Think about what the space needs to do for you and go from there.

THOUGHTS ON STORAGE?

One of the most overlooked potential storage spaces in your kitchen is right at your feet. Take advantage of the rarely used toe-kick under bottom cabinets by installing shallow drawers to store platters, pots and pans, baking sheets, trash bags, grocery sacks, and much more. Outfit the drawer with a touch-latch release so it can be easily opened with a tap of your foot. And don't forget about the top of the cabinets, which have ample space to set up attractive storage boxes for seasonal items and other cookware that is not often used. Another under-utilized space is the gap between cabinets and appliances. Installing a pullout pilaster can conceal kitchen essentials such as dishtowels, oven mitts, and spices. If there's room in your kitchen, install an island for some counter space that doubles as a great storage area.

TOP RIGHT: Splashes of color create a sense of drama in the formal dining room.

BOTTOM RIGHT: Imbued with a blend of antiques, reproductions, and one-of-a-kind pieces, the dining room is steeped in traditional style.

FACING PAGE: Clean lines combine with bold accents and playful patterns in the rug and chairs to create a cool, contemporary vibe.
Photographs by Mark Herron Photography

Gearheart Construction

Build the relationship, then the house.

Gearheart Construction works in the traditional general contracting model with skilled project managers and carpenters involved through every phase of the homebuilding process. Many relationships between the firm's leadership and homeowners, architects, designers, and venders span nearly 50 years. Gearheart's first effort goes into being a team member in designing, estimating, handling construction administration, and contracting the residence. It also has a fully staffed maintenance company to ensure that the homes it builds are kept in pristine condition. The firm works with the best architects and designers in the area to help owners achieve the specific look they want. Consequently, Gearheart has no signature design. The only common denominators in the firm's work are high standards and relationships that last for decades.

LEFT: Neutral colors and beautiful materials make the high-end kitchen a restful space.
Photograph courtesy of Gearheart Construction

KITCHEN INSPIRATION

ONE THING TO KEEP IN MIND CONCERNING CONSTRUCTION?
The kitchen is one of the most used areas in the home, so choose
quality materials and have them professionally installed.

RENOVATION CONSIDERATIONS?
Just as the exterior needs to look like it belongs in its neighborhood,
the new kitchen needs to look like it belongs in the house. That could
mean renovating the adjoining areas or simply being mindful of the
existing style, materials, and construction methods.

ABOVE: The bold color of the cabinetry and trimwork expresses the
homeowners' vibrant personalities. The composition is grounded by stainless
steel elements: shelving, backsplash, appliances, and island countertop.

RIGHT: The large island with asymmetrical overhang serves as the focal
point of the contemporary kitchen.

FACING PAGE TOP: Appealing yet unexpected materials and colors
combine for a unique design that looks as if it has always been there.

FACING PAGE BOTTOM: Maintaining clean lines is the key to classic design.
Photographs courtesy of Gearheart Construction

Grandeur Design

Luxury makes a house a home.

Brenda Blaylock always knew she was destined for the design industry, while Susan Semmelmann took a more circuitous route—via elementary education and then aviation—to find her true passion. The two were introduced rather serendipitously and three showrooms later, they have earned quite a reputation in the design world. Being commissioned for whole-house designs and single-room renovations is certainly a primary interest, though they serve an even broader clientele. Their Grandeur Design showrooms attract professional designers and decorators who appreciate the curated selection of furniture and accessories as well as do-it-yourselfers looking for unique items to personalize their homes. What unites all of their creative efforts is a decided focus on high-end design. Offering services and pieces in a range of styles, they are particularly known for taking the cherished Old World style to a new level of luxury.

TOP LEFT: Crisp lines and beautiful finishes create a contemporary-chic aesthetic.

BOTTOM LEFT: The traditional design is clean and fresh.

FACING PAGE: The beautifully detailed kitchen embodies French country *elegance*.
Photographs courtesy of Grandeur Design

Ingean Construction

Functional designs should be based on individual styles.

Since 1996, Brad Inge has been building lasting relationships with his clients—literally—as he oversees high-quality construction for everything from new home builds to complex renovations and expansions. In addition to being a relationship-based contractor, Brad harbors experience in commercial, residential, and kitchens as well as a diversified skill set including woodwork, painting, and more. Discovering creative ways to execute visions to the utmost is of high priority with Ingean Construction, as the company's team delivers functionality combined with an impressive display of the client's individual style. Brad works with talented design firms, combining their vision with his experience to capture an end result that is precisely what the owner and architect expected. With each design, Brad focuses on three key elements—order, process, and balance—that enable him to produce a space that translates well for any style, be it traditional, modern, or minimalist. This flexible trait makes him a high-valued commodity and results in successful designs for all styles of life.

LEFT: The builder skillfully interpreted and executed the owner's program and Turner Boaz Architecture's design.
Photographs by Stacy Luecker Photography

Jonn Spradlin Design

Everyone needs a gentle nudge to stretch their design aesthetic.

Even more than an experienced designer, Jonn Spradlin is a stellar communicator. He finds it important to help homeowners make design choices that stretch their sense of style. Clients always appreciate the level of customization in Jonn's designs, and he enjoys hearing how well his homes suit people's needs and lifestyles. Jonn goes to great lengths to help owners get an accurate picture in their heads about the project, and he does this with vivid three-dimensional renderings. Jonn's intentionally boutique firm means that he is personally involved with every project and can tailor all aspects of the design. He's as concerned with the functional as with the aesthetic. He makes certain to incorporate the latest technology and materials in the spaces where people spend the majority of their lives; these rooms should make people feel special. Creating a visually appealing environment that enhances lives—fewer steps to take, doors to open, buttons to push—making the homeowners proud and feel good, that's Jonn's mark of a successful project.

TOP LEFT: The doors and cabinetry were made on-site with reclaimed flooring from a riverfront warehouse in St. Louis.
Photograph by Sam Smead

BOTTOM LEFT: Wonderful textures, interesting lines, and natural materials are the ingredients of timeless design.
Photograph by Susan Guice

FACING PAGE: The Texas Mediterranean hacienda kitchen features a hand-sculpted relief behind the stove and a beautifully hand-painted ceiling.
Photograph by Sam Smead

Lee Lormand Design

Innovation, editing, and style are the basic fundamentals of interiors.

With projects that often combine elements of the classic and the modern, Lee Lormand creates custom designed interiors that are well-edited and distinctively statement-making. Formally establishing his eponymous firm in 2008, he has worked in the design industry since 1998. While Lee's experience spans an eclectic range of projects including showrooms, retail spaces, hotels, and restaurants, he specializes in residential design. His meticulous eye for detail and personal attention ensures that each project—no matter how large or small—is crafted and curated to reflect the dreams and individuality of the client. Lee is passionate about assembling the best elements of design into a thoughtful collaboration with the client while engaging with an extensive network of artisans and professionals to ensure that the exact vision and styling is achieved. As a Registered Interior Designer, Lee offers a full range of services including all aspects of interior design as well as interior architecture and custom furniture design.

TOP LEFT, BOTTOM LEFT, & FACING PAGE: Sleek surfaces in warm neutrals and a splash of vibrant color were used to create the backdrop in this kitchen-living space in a downtown Dallas high rise. The space includes a breakfast niche with a custom designed banquette seat and custom floating cantilevered shelves with LED lights.
Photographs by Lee Lormand

L. Lumpkins, Architect

Comfortable living areas encourage meaningful interaction.

A classic look with a comfortable déjà vu quality. When Lloyd Lumpkins can achieve this in his designs, he's a proud architect with delighted homeowners. Lloyd credits a somewhat unlikely combination of historical architecture—buildings he has experienced in his native East Texas and in Europe and Asia where he regularly travels—as the inspiration for his work. He appreciates the romantic quality of Revival-style homes from the early 1900s and is enamored with the eclectic nature of long-established cities abroad. While his portfolio embodies the timelessness and intrigue of older structures, Lloyd designs expressly for the here and now. He is attuned to what modern families want and need in order to love their homes and make day-to-day tasks all the more pleasant. To this end, he works hard to ensure that his clients understand how each space will look and feel as well as he does. Vivid three-dimensional drawings, careful explanations, and meaningful dialogue with the future residents are key parts of his creative process.

LEFT: Traditional with a contemporary edge, the Hamptons-style kitchen incorporates polished white marble and adjustable polished silver wall sconces.
Photograph by Michael Hunter

KITCHEN INSPIRATION

UNIQUE WAYS YOU'VE PERSONALIZED A KITCHEN?
We designed an inglenook by an oversized cooking fireplace as a fun gathering area to make popcorn, toast nuts, or roast marshmallows on cool evenings.

MOST IMPORTANT DESIGN ELEMENT?
Reinforcing the idea of hearth and home. The kitchen is a gathering place where family memories are made. Layouts that incorporate these principles encourage social interactions.

FAVORITE LOOK?
Hidden appliances and spaces that are loaded with windows.

TOP LEFT: The French Arcadian-style home features salvaged timber beams and lots of natural light.
Photograph by Shoot-2-Sell

BOTTOM LEFT: The classic French country kitchen has a brick herringbone ceiling. Table lamps make the island feel like a piece of furniture.
Photograph by Lloyd Lumpkins

FACING PAGE: Designed like an Italian villa, the kitchen features a beamed ceiling with rolled brick detailing and a metal hood over the range.
Photograph by Michael Hunter

Malone Maxwell
Borson Architects

Deliberate design is how dreams are realized.

At Malone Maxwell Borson Architects, each design is formulated as a background to the client's life. It must match up to their personalities and lifestyles perfectly and never interfere or overshadow them, but rather support their enthusiasms in every aspect. Audrey Maxwell and Bob Borson oversee the Dallas-based firm—established in 1992—alongside founding principal Michael Malone, who also serves as president of the Texas Society of Architects and is a contributing editor to *Texas Architect* magazine. The firm's passion for perfection is evident in its very deliberate design process, including drawings and sketches that not only portray the potential space but also describe and imply its character. Thus clients are able to envision it more fully and also impart their own creative input, which results in a strong sense of personal satisfaction. Detailed finishes, simple materials, and luminous colors result in timeless design and beautiful space solutions.

TOP LEFT: The great room opens directly to the kitchen, creating one large space for living and entertaining.

BOTTOM LEFT: A large front porch sets the tone for the open and welcoming house.

FACING PAGE: The kitchen is bright and cheerful and features two islands, one for food preparation, the other a scullery.
Photographs by Jud Haggard Photography

New Life Hardwoods
History is beautiful.

New Life Hardwoods serves a dual purpose: bestowing gorgeous flooring on deserving architecture and preserving centuries' old species for future generations. The specialty company offers a wide array of beautifully finished species: oak, pine, walnut, cherry, cypress, poplar, maple, and chestnut. It reclaims old-growth wood from a variety of sources, including old buildings, landfills, and rivers across North America, and then re-mills the material into high-end flooring, walls, and furniture. Thousands of acres of long-leaf pine, for instance, were harvested in the late 1800s from forests in Texas and Louisiana that were home to giants up to 12 feet in diameter, 175 feet tall, and 400 years old. Even rarer species are recovered from deep within the silt of rivers like the Chatahouchee; the discovery process is time-consuming yet worth the effort for remarkably preserved 600-year-old treasures. The exceptional characteristics of reclaimed wood—its weight, density, dimensions, patina, and age—tell stories from long ago, and you don't need to be a history buff to appreciate the wonder and intrinsic value of such a material.

TOP LEFT, BOTTOM LEFT, & FACING PAGE: Walking on reclaimed hardwood floors is like touching a piece of history—and the aesthetic is beyond compare.
Photographs by Allan Akins

Olsen Studios

Inventive design makes life comfortable.

It's typical for clients to deal with multiple consultants when it comes to home projects, whether new builds or renovations. But at Olsen Studios, clients are able to enjoy a literal one-stop-shop. Established by Jamie Olsen Ali, Olsen Studios focuses on one important key concept: creativity. Architecture and interior design co-exist, created to complement each other throughout the entire process. So when it comes to devising the perfect kitchen, homeowners are able to carefully work through architectural details, from site planning to construction documents, with the studio's pros. Once the bones of the space are in place, clients move on to interior design. The team at Olsen excels at budgeting, producing conceptual packages for clients to get an idea of the big picture and also select the best furniture and finishes that complement their style. There are also remodeling experts on hand, and Olsen Studios touts a Studio Selects program that focuses on smaller architectural and interior design projects—like updating a kitchen with a dreamy island space, serene marble countertops, and an envy-inducing industrial stove top range. It's all clever design from top to bottom, start to finish.

LEFT: The cozy farmhouse kitchen features white oak floors, painted shaker cabinetry, quartz counters, brass hardware, and concrete octagonal tiles from Anne Sacks.
Photograph by Shoot 2 Sell Photography

LEFT: Ebonized oak cabinetry, quartz countertops and mixed porcelain and glass accent tile from Knoxtile come together to create the modern butler's pantry/bar.
Photograph by Michael Hunter Interior Photography

ABOVE: A true chef's dream, the modern farmhouse kitchen features white oak floors, ebonized oak cabinets, and a concrete apron farmhouse sink.
Photograph by Michael Hunter Interior Photography

FACING PAGE TOP: Surrounded by glass walls, the stunning dining space is filled with natural light and views of the nearby farmhouse-style pavilions.
Photograph by Shoot 2 Sell Photography

FACING PAGE BOTTOM: The bistro-style breakfast nook includes a leather and rustic wood bench and iron pedestal table. The design dictated a durable space for children, yet elegant enough for a candlelit dinner.
Photograph by Shoot 2 Sell Photography

KITCHEN INSPIRATION

BEST WAY TO BEGIN A REDESIGN?
Seriously study the end user. Whether the project is a remodel or new construction, we like to ask the clients to prepare a meal for us in their current kitchen. Carefully observing this process will reveal how the space will be used and what the most important aspects of the design will be. Some kitchens may only serve to entertain and gather, while others need to be workhorses for some serious cooking.

FAVORITE KITCHEN GADGET?
An insta-hot water dispenser. I insist on them for all clients. While they are fantastic for the obvious quick hot tea or cocoa, there are countless uses for instant boiling water—think defrost, rapid boil, hot towels.

WHAT MAKES A KITCHEN DREAMY?
Abundant natural light, a beautiful view, easy access to the outdoors, a great sound system, and a cozy spot to enjoy a glass of wine.

Studio Thomas James

Designers should be chameleons of style.

Philip Vanderford and Jason Jones love a good challenge. They have designed in a variety of settings, including California wine country, the Rocky Mountains, the British West Indies, Paris, Shanghai, and of course their home base in Dallas. They have a natural ability to quickly get up to speed on the cultural nuances of locale and the logistics of completing installations in geographically complex settings. Formally educated in interior design, Philip and Jason are also experienced in the world of construction, which gives them a rare perspective that everyone appreciates. They are as excited about the way a space functions as the way it looks, careful to consider every aspect of a project. In order to ensure that every detail is meticulously executed, they maintain an in-house workroom that produces custom upholstery, window coverings, furniture, and other specialty pieces of exquisite quality in a very reasonable timeframe. Most of Philip and Jason's time is devoted to full-house interior design, whether working from the ground up or doing a major renovation, but they do a fair amount of single-room remodels. Expressing their love of aesthetic perfection, they also uniquely offer one-day makeovers to give homeowners the opportunity for a fresh look—fast—that is full of style.

LEFT: The crisp kitchen is centered on a custom stainless hood and polished nickel industrial fixtures. Antique blue and white porcelain, custom sea grass rugs bound in leather, and soft blue paint draw you in with their warmth. The contrast of the contemporary stools keeps the space fresh and relevant.
Photographs by RUDA Photography

KITCHEN INSPIRATION

EVERY KITCHEN DESIGN MUST INCLUDE?
Warmth! Today our kitchens are not only places to prepare food, but also the center of day-to-day living. Kitchens must be every bit as inviting as traditional living spaces.

WHAT'S ONE TIME YOU SAVED THE DAY?
We were working on a grand mountain home that required sourcing antiques from around the world. Our client ran across a chandelier that seemingly checked all the boxes, but since we weren't there to review it, we insisted that the client have the piece appraised by an independent resource. The appraiser told us that the chandelier was not a priceless antique but rather a well-crafted reproduction. We saved our client from making a very expensive mistake, and it was a huge turning point in our relationship.

CREATIVE WAYS TO CUSTOMIZE A KITCHEN?
Mix up your materials. Varying your finishes and stones gives an evolved look that reads sophisticated and interesting. The other benefit is that spaces will tend to have an enduring classic aesthetic that transcends trends.

THOUGHTS ON REFINISHING VERSUS REPLACING?
We're always fans of refinishing anything of quality. Refinishing can breathe new life into cabinetry and is truly the ultimate form of recycling.

TOP: The new home feels evolved with the addition of a rich custom copper hood accented with brass strapping. The pot rack serves as a perfect place for an avid chef to display her collection of antique copper pots. Pale blue paint carries throughout the home and allows for an excellent contrast against the exposed beams.

BOTTOM: The classic 1920s home was renovated to incorporate a breakfast area in the kitchen, which features a generous island fitted with a mitered Calacatta marble top. Antique copper lanterns and reproduced original moldings allow the renovated area to flow seamlessly into the home.

FACING PAGE: The generous dark alder island has a mitered stone top executed out of Macaubas quartzite. The custom stainless hood is set off by dark strapping and polished nickel screws. Custom light fixtures complement the space with a high level of refinement down to their painted gray finish and studded strapping. The space is kept warm with the contrast of dark honed marble and pale green paint on the ceiling.
Photographs by RUDA Photography

Symmetry Architects
Open collaboration makes for great architecture.

Architecture is, by design, a collaborative process. Since 1998 Clint Pearson, principal architect of Symmetry Architects, has collaborated with homeowners, builders, and designers to create noteworthy homes across the state and beyond. Clint invests his creativity and passion into learning about this clients' vision of the perfect home, and his reputation speaks for itself. From French and English-inspired designs to Mediterranean homes and abodes that epitomize the Texas Hill Country, Clint's portfolio is acclaimed and highly awarded. But it is the personal connection that Clint makes with his clientele that is the motivating factor behind his work. There is never any doubt that Clint is building a home to support a unique lifestyle. He and his team are dedicated to upholding the distinctive signature of both homeowners and the homes themselves. The result is a collection of homes that evoke warmth and a true sense of home.

LEFT: This gorgeous kitchen has an understated elegance achieved by clean simple lines and an abundance of natural light. The central focus is on the cooking area which features a zinc hood and Noblesse 2 tiled wall by Tabarka Studios, selected by Laura Lee Clark Interiors. Behind the kitchen is a scullery, which removes the visual clutter and mess from the primary kitchen space.
Photograph by Brad Taylor Imaging

TOP LEFT, TOP RIGHT, & BOTTOM RIGHT: This functional kitchen integrates a beverage center in one corner. ninety-degree corner windows introduce plenty of natural light and provide views into a inviting courtyard at the front of the residence. The dining room beyond is entered through a deep arched opening, which is flanked by Gaggenau wine columns.

FACING PAGE: The homeowners both have a passion for the culinary arts, so naturally they needed their own islands by Downsview Kitchen. His island evokes a rugged, masculine feel with the use of walnut wood and satin brass hardware. Her island balances the space with the use of a grey lacquer base cabinet capped with Carrara white marble containing delicate grey veining. A backdrop of colorful geometric backsplash from Ann Sacks, selected by Brown Design Group, and a 60-inch La Cornue range, set the stage for performing the art of cooking. The scene is lit from above by gloss black and brass pendant lights from Charles Edwards of London.
Photographs by HW Homes

KITCHEN INSPIRATION

WHAT MUST EVERY KITCHEN INCLUDE?
Natural light and an efficient layout.

DIFFERENT WAYS KITCHENS NEED TO FUNCTION?
My recent kitchen designs have included a scullery or a chef's pantry. The scullery, a relic from old European kitchens, is typically tucked away behind the kitchen and is used primarily as a place to wash and store dishes, pots, etc. It can also serve as a staging area for caterers. The chef's pantry provides a place to store small appliances, etc. which frees up counter space in the kitchen. These two spaces allow us to remove the mess and visual clutter from the kitchen proper. It is very important when entertaining, since everyone typically congregates in the kitchen. The scullery and chef's pantry allow the host and their guests to focus on enjoying the art of preparing food in a beautifully designed setting.

TOP & BOTTOM RIGHT: This spacious kitchen with 12-foot-tall ceilings and stained timber beams is anchored by an oversized island topped with Calcutta gold marble.

FACING PAGE: A brick arch adds color and texture in contrast to the overall soft contemporary feel of this space, as well as delineating the kitchen from the family room. The informal dining area of this kitchen connects to a small inglenook with an antique limestone fireplace, creating a cozy space for mother and daughter conversations.
Photographs by Brad Taylor Imaging

Tiffany McKinzie
Interior Design

Your home represents the best of you.

Tiffany McKinzie believes that a home is more than the sum of its parts. It's about emotion, history, experiences, love, comfort. A home tells a very personal story. A story of the lives of the people who inhabit it. Whether grandiose or modest, newly constructed or recently restored, its livelihood is a result of the people who reside within its four walls. Tiffany's job is to understand her clients' passions, desires, and tastes and translate them into their surroundings. This creates the vision for the home and drives the design, flow, features, and materials. Tiffany guides the homeowner through every stage of construction and assists with each decision that must be made: framing, plumbing, electrical, flooring, cabinetry, lighting, colors, textures, and more. It is Tiffany's desire that her clients' homes inspire them and leave them feeling content; that their homes represent the best of them. Then she knows that she has successfully told their story.

TOP LEFT, BOTTOM LEFT, & FACING PAGE: This beautifully appointed kitchen would make any chef giddy. It features a bevy of top notch Miele appliances including a combi-steam oven, convection speed oven, built-in coffee maker, refrigeration, and much more. The custom range hood, which features a black crocodile texture, is a major focal point and also grounds the lofty ceilings. Visual Comfort pendants hang over the marble and butcher block top island.
Photographs by AMWZ Photography

Traci Connell Interiors

Classic modern is always in style.

Known for her refreshing perspective on design and timeless sense of style, Traci Connell takes a unique approach to realizing each interior. Pairing state-of-the-art project management systems with decades of firsthand design experience, she and her team are able to track with remarkable accuracy the timeframes and overall progress of a project. This gives homeowners peace of mind that the design will be beautiful and completed smoothly, with as few surprises as possible. Traci absolutely loves the creative process, and being efficient with time and resources allows her to spend the vast majority of her energy on the design itself, from space planning to architectural detailing, furniture design, and the appointment of fixtures, fabrics, and finishes. Transitional interior designs that combine modern lines and classic styles are somewhat of a specialty, though Traci is delighted at the opportunity to be inspired by homeowners' interests and tastes.

TOP LEFT: Nestled within the curved kitchen wall, the banquette is perfect for casual dining.

BOTTOM LEFT: The mosaic backsplash was custom made from a combination of natural stones. The beautifully finished hood perfectly caps off the professional-grade stove.

FACING PAGE: Transitional architectural details create an impact in the large-scale kitchen and keeping room.
Photographs by Michael Hunter

The Water Closet

Good design is timeless design.

The perfect fixture makes the best interior design even better. When trying to figure out how on earth to allocate resources, professionals often advocate splurging on the elements that will be touched daily. It makes all-too-much sense. Deciding on those perfect somethings, however, is a another matter. The Water Closet is Caryn Evans' haven of high-end perfection, where designer lines and options for customization abound— plumbing fixtures, cabinetry, bath products, tile, accessories, and more. Design professionals are on hand to help people zero in on the finishing touches that will make their hearts sing. While the specialty showroom is certainly a claim to fame, Caryn and her team also offer comprehensive interior design services, from start-to-finish project management with turnkey design and construction to hourly consultation. Their willingness to partner with clients on such a wide range of projects gives them wonderful insight and keeps the door wide open for future collaboration. Adept at designing traditional and contemporary alike, Caryn describes her appealing signature style as warm, intimate, and infused with avant-garde materials. Each project benefits from Caryn's unique background in architecture, interior design, and vintage detailing as well as her innate love of helping others discover their sense of style.

TOP LEFT & FACING PAGE: A classic Tudor with a hint of rustic flair, the home features elegant finishes and graceful lines.

BOTTOM LEFT: Contemporary elements provide a touch of the unexpected in the Texas vernacular-style home.
Photographs by Clementine Grace

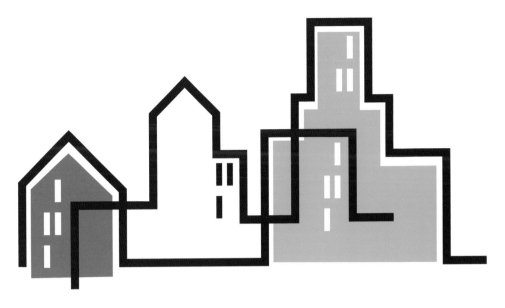

D W E L L *with* D I G N I T Y

In November, Dwell with Dignity partnered with Rebuilding Together Greater Dallas on a Homes for Heroes project for an Army veteran and her two daughters. This mom was injured while on duty, and upon her return, she found herself living in a home that was literally falling apart. The ceiling in the girls' bedroom had caved in, the floors had fallen through, there were holes on the side of the house, the stairs were collapsing, and they had no working plumbing. She and the girls had been using a neighbor's restroom for the past year. But this sweet woman didn't give up, and even though she was working two jobs, every repair was out of reach.

That's when DwD and Rebuilding Together came in! RTGD completely rebuilt the structure, fixed the plumbing and installed central air. "Teaming with Rebuilding Together gave us a pristine blank slate in which we could create a warm and inviting home, complete with everything they needed to move forward with less stress and more pride," said DwD Founder and President, Lisa Robison.

The living area of the home is a combination of calming and inviting blues and greens. The girls' bedroom is a purple and

pink haven reflecting their interests. With this new home, the stress and chaos that existed before is alleviated, and they can now focus on building a new future and can actually begin to realize some of the goals they set long ago.

We often take the simplest things in life for granted, but those things are now a reality for this resilient family. We think the youngest said it best, "I'm having a play date every day!"

Signature
Publishing Group

www.signatureboutiquebooks.com

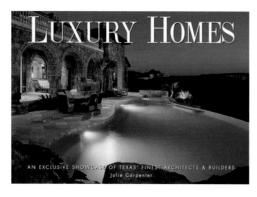

LUXURY HOMES
AN EXCLUSIVE SHOWCASE OF TEXAS' FINEST ARCHITECTS & BUILDERS
Jolie Carpenter

Beautiful Weddings
OF TEXAS
CELEBRATION INSPIRATION
JOLIE CARPENTER

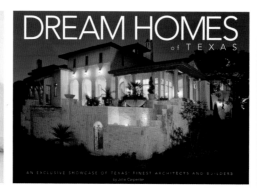

DREAM HOMES
of TEXAS
AN EXCLUSIVE SHOWCASE OF TEXAS' FINEST ARCHITECTS AND BUILDERS
by Jolie Carpenter

Spectacular Weddings
of Texas
A COLLECTION OF TEXAS WEDDINGS AND LOVE STORIES

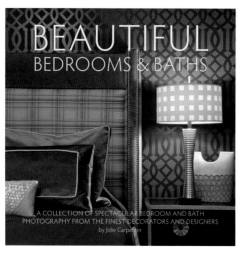

BEAUTIFUL
BEDROOMS & BATHS
A COLLECTION OF SPECTACULAR BEDROOM AND BATH
PHOTOGRAPHY FROM THE FINEST DECORATORS AND DESIGNERS
by Jolie Carpenter

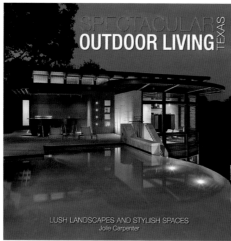

SPECTACULAR
OUTDOOR LIVING TEXAS
LUSH LANDSCAPES AND STYLISH SPACES
Jolie Carpenter

Beautiful Homes
of Texas
AN EXCLUSIVE COLLECTION OF THE FINEST DESIGNERS IN TEXAS
by Jolie Carpenter

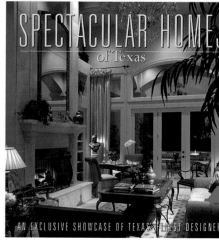

SPECTACULAR HOMES
of Texas
AN EXCLUSIVE SHOWCASE OF TEXAS' FINEST DESIGNER

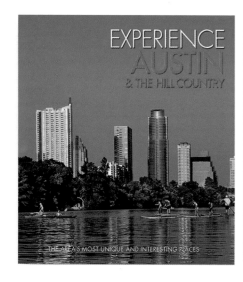

EXPERIENCE
AUSTIN
& THE HILL COUNTRY
THE AREA'S MOST UNIQUE AND INTERESTING PLACES

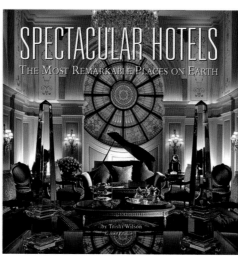

SPECTACULAR HOTELS
THE MOST REMARKABLE PLACES ON EARTH
by Trisha Wilson

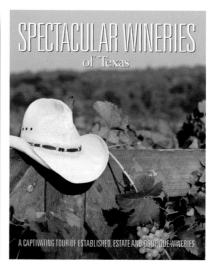

SPECTACULAR WINERIES
of Texas
A CAPTIVATING TOUR OF ESTABLISHED, ESTATE AND BOUTIQUE WINERIES

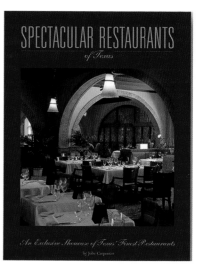

SPECTACULAR RESTAURANTS
of Texas
An Exclusive Showcase of Texas' Finest Restaurants
by Jolie Carpenter